A GUIDE TO G

The SPCK International Study Guides incorporate the much loved and respected TEF series, and follow the tradition of: clarity and simplicity; a worldwide, ecumenical perspective; and an emphasis on application of the material studied, drawing out its relevance for Christians today. The Guides are ideal for first year students and Bible study groups, as well as for multi-cultural classes, and students for whom English is a second language.

SPCK International Study Guide 28

A GUIDE TO GALATIANS

David H. van Daalen

First published in Great Britain 1990
SPCK
Holy Trinity Church
Marylebone Road
London NW1 4DU

Third impression 1997

Unless otherwise stated, the Scripture quotations in this publication are
from the Revised Standard Version of the Bible, Ecumenical Edition
Copyright 1973 by the Division of Christian Education
of the National Council of the Churches of Christ in the USA.

The photographs are reproduced by courtesy of Mark Edwards
(pp. 35a and b, 53a, 83) and Camera Press Limited.

British Library Cataloguing-in-Publication Data
A catalogue record for this book is available from
The British Library

ISBN 0-281-04502-X

Printed in Great Britain by
Latimer Trend & Company Ltd, Plymouth

Contents

Preface

As a work of this kind owes much to the work of others, I wish to express my gratitude to many people who have written about the Letter to the Galatians, mentioning in particular F. F. Bruce, E. de Witt Burton, H. Lietzmann, H. Schlier, K. L. Schmidt and P. A. van Stempfoort. I also wish to thank Dr Stuart Blanch and Dr John Roxborough, who read the first draft of my MS and gave some valuable comments; and the Rev. Nicholas Beddow and Miss Daphne Terry, whose assistance has been invaluable.

DAVID H. VAN DAALEN

Using this Guide

The plan of this Guide follows much the same pattern as that of other biblical Guides in the series.

In his *Introduction* the author sets the scene for our study of Paul's Letter to the Galatians by providing a brief note on its background, and on the relationship between Paul's letters to Churches and Luke's account of his ministry in the Acts of the Apostles. In the light of understanding gained from close study of the Letter, the *Postscript* sums up Paul's purpose in writing and the arguments he used against the misteaching which was causing a rift in the Galatian Church, and hindering its development. Finally, it points to the significance of the Letter for the life of the Church today.

Study of the letter itself has been divided into short sections according to natural breaks in the text. But before beginning their work readers may find it helpful to consider how they can make the best use of this Guide.

Each section consists of:

1. A *Summary* of the passage, briefly indicating the subject-matter it contains. Of course the summary is not intended as a substitute for the words of the Bible itself, which need to be read very carefully at each stage of our study.

2. *Notes* on particular words and points of possible difficulty, especially as relating to Paul's purpose in writing, and to the situation of conflict which had arisen.

3. An *Interpretation* of the passage and the teaching it contained, both as it applied to those to whom it was addressed, and as we should understand and apply it to our own situation today.

SPECIAL NOTES

The four Special Notes, on Grace, Faith according to Paul, Righteousness and Justification, and The Law, have been separated from the sections dealing directly with the text, partly because of their length, and partly because each relates to more than one section.

STUDY SUGGESTIONS AND QUESTIONS

Suggestions for further study and review are included at the end of each section. Besides enabling students working alone to check their own progress, they provide subjects for individual and group research, and topics for discussion. They are of four main sorts:

1. *Word Study*, to help readers check and deepen their understanding of important words and phrases.
2. *Review of Content*, to help readers check the work they have done, and make sure they have fully grasped the ideas and points of teaching given.
3. *Bible Study*, to relate Paul's ideas and teaching in the Letter with related ideas and teaching in other parts of the Bible.
4. *Discussion and Application*, to help readers think out the practical significance of Paul's words, both to those to whom he was writing, and for the life and work of the Churches and of individual Christians in the modern situation. Many of these are suitable for use in a group as well as for students working alone.

The best way to use these Study Suggestions is: first, re-read the Bible passage; second, read the appropriate section of the Guide once or twice; and then do the work suggested, either in writing or in group discussion, without looking at the Guide again unless instructed to do so.

The *Key to Study Suggestions* at the end of the Guide will enable you to check your work on those questions which can be checked in this way. In most cases the Key does not give the answer to a question: it shows where an answer is to be found.

Please note that all these suggestions are only *suggestions*. Some readers may not wish to use them. Some teachers may wish to select only those most relevant to the needs of their particular students, or may wish to substitute questions of their own.

A list of books suggested for *further reading* is provided at the end of this Note, and a *map* of the countries around the Eastern Mediterranean at the time when Paul was writing.

INDEX

The Index includes only the more important names of people and places and the main subjects treated in the Letter or discussed in the Guide. Bold-type page references are provided to show where particular subjects are treated in detail.

BIBLE VERSION

The English translation of the Bible used in the Guide is the *Revised Standard Version Common Bible* (Ecumenical Edition) (RSV). Reference is also made to the *New English Bible* and *Revised English Bible* (NEB, REB), the *New International Version* (NIV), the *Jerusalem Bible* and *New Jerusalem Bible* (JB, NJB), and the *Good News Bible* (GNB or TEV), where these help to show the meaning more clearly, and in one or two cases to the *Authorized* (King James) *Version* (AV).

FURTHER READING

INTRODUCTORY BOOKS

William Barclay, *Galatians and Ephesians* (Daily Study Bible). Edinburgh, St Andrew Press.

Alan Cole, *Galatians* (Tynedale Commentaries). Nottingham, Inter-Varsity Press.

H. P. Homan, *Galatians*. Adelaide, Lutheran Publishing House 1976.

A. M. Hunter, *Galatians, Ephesians, Philippians and Colossians* (Layman's Bible Commentary). Atlanta, John Knox Press.

Hugh Montefiore, *Paul the Apostle*. London, Collins 1981.

William Neil, *Galatians* (Cambridge Bible Commentaries). Cambridge University Press.

MORE ADVANCED BOOKS

F. F. Bruce, *Paul: Apostle of the Free Spirit*. Exeter, Paternoster 1977.

Chas B. Cousar, *Galatians*. Atlanta, John Knox Press.

Y. K. Fung, *The Epistle to the Galatians* (New International Commentary on the New Testament). Grand Rapids, Eerdmans/Exeter, Paternoster 1989.

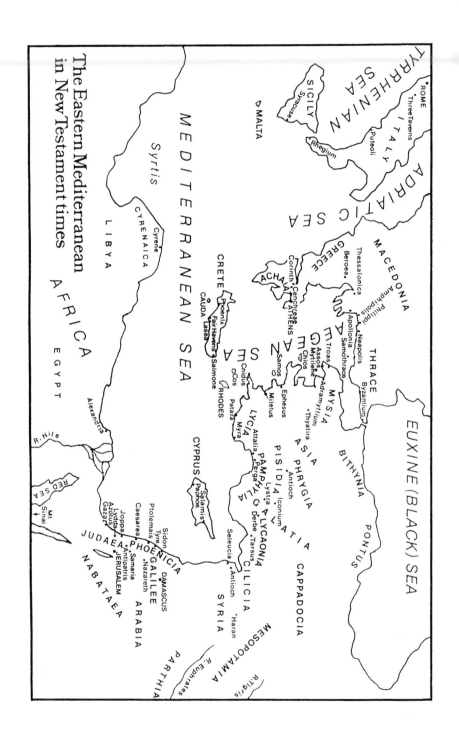

The Eastern Mediterranean in New Testament times

Introduction

THE LETTER AND ITS WRITER

The Letter to the Galatians is one of the earliest writings of the New Testament, and, though it is short, it is a very important work. It was written by the Apostle Paul, who also wrote the Letters to the Romans, the Corinthians and Philemon, probably those to the Philippians and Thessalonians, and perhaps those to the Colossians, the Ephesians, Timothy and Titus.

Paul's ministry is recorded in the Acts of the Apostles (Acts 9; 11.25–30; 12.25; 13—28). However, we must be careful in our use of the Acts as a guide to Paul's life and teaching. When Luke wrote the Acts, he wanted to tell about the progress of the gospel from Jerusalem to what he called the furthest parts of the earth, meaning western Europe (see Acts 1.8). Paul played a large part in this, so Luke paid a lot of attention to Paul and his work. But Luke was more interested in the Church as a whole than in the biographies of individual people, and Paul was not the 'hero' of his book.

Luke's purpose is shown clearly in the sermons and speeches which take up about a third of his book. No one took shorthand notes, when these were spoken. Some people may have remembered much of what had been said, for people who do not read are often good listeners, and have good memories, but they would not have been able to give a precise word-for-word record. It was Luke who gave these sermons the form which they have in the Acts. That explains why there is so little difference between the preaching of Paul and that of Peter recorded there. In Luke's view that did not matter; what he wanted to show was that they both preached the gospel, without stressing that each did so in his own way. To Luke the important thing about Paul was not so much that he travelled all over the Roman Empire, but that he did so in order to spread the gospel. Luke's account of Paul's travels gives us a marvellous and interesting picture of his ministry; the sermons show that this was a ministry of the *gospel*. They show the gospel as Luke had received it from Paul and the other apostles, but not the particular way in which Paul presented it. The good news has been, and still is, presented in many different forms. The New Testament reflects this variety, and so shows the many riches of the gospel. The Acts show us Luke's presentation, as does Luke's Gospel, and our knowledge of Christ would be much poorer if we did not have his presentation. But it would also be much poorer if we did not have those of Matthew, Mark,

1

John, James or Paul, and for Paul's presentation we must rely above all on his own writings.

Even here we must remember that Paul's writings are letters, written in view of particular circumstances. All of them were addressed to people who were already Christians, and some of the letters, including this one, were to people Paul knew or churches he had already visited. In each case he wrote what the occasion demanded, and we should not expect them to provide a handbook of Christian doctrine, nor try to draw too far-reaching conclusions from what he did not write. For example, Paul said little about Jesus's earthly life, and some people have thought that he did not know much about that, or did not think it very important. But we do not really know how much or little he knew: he could certainly have asked other Christians all he wanted to know. Nor do we know how much Paul told his Churches about Jesus's ministry. He may have told them a great deal, but we just do not know. What we do know is that the institution of the Lord's Supper, Jesus's death on the Cross, and His resurrection were events which he had to mention in his letters. In Paul's days writing was a time-consuming job, and paper was very expensive, so people kept their letters short. Paul's letters are among the longest known from the ancient world, but even he would not have cared to write more than he needed to.

So the Letter to the Galatians was a real letter, written on a particular occasion, to specific people, and in view of particular circumstances. What those circumstances were, we can only find out from the letter itself, and we shall discuss them as matters arise. But what Paul wrote was always important. He always saw the deeper significance of events and people's reactions to them, and what he wrote is never trivial. In responding to the situation in the Galatian Churches, he dug down right to the root of the matter. This letter is not just an interesting historical document from which we can learn something about a small part of the history of the early Church; it has a lasting significance, and contains much that we need to relate to the context of our own lives and apply in our own Churches.

STUDY SUGGESTIONS

REVIEW OF CONTENT

1. 'Paul's ministry is recorded in the Acts of the Apostles' (p. 1). Explain why we should be careful in our use of the Acts as a guide to Paul's life and teaching.
2. What did Luke regard as the most important thing about Paul's ministry?
3. 'The Acts show us Luke's presentation of the gospel' (p. 1).

    (a) What was Luke's chief aim in writing the Acts?

    (b) Where must we look for Paul's presentation of the gospel?

4. Give two reasons why we should not expect Paul's letters to provide a handbook of Christian doctrine.

BIBLE STUDY

5. As a background to study of Paul's letter to the Galatians, read the following passages in Acts: 8.1–17, 25; 9.1–31; 10; 11. Then write a short account (not more than 500 words), telling how Paul became a Christian, and what led to his becoming a missionary to the Gentiles.

DISCUSSION AND APPLICATION

6. What is meant by the statement that 'All Christian teaching is "contextual", i.e. related to real-life situations? See p. 2, para. 2. How far do you agree? Give your reasons.

7. 'The good news has been presented, and is presented today, in many different forms' (p. 1). What effect might such differences have on people seeking for the first time to learn about the Christian faith?

1.1–5
Greeting

SUMMARY

Paul, stressing that he is an apostle, greets the Churches of Galatia, conveying to them grace and peace from God the Father and Jesus Christ.

NOTES

1.1. An apostle. The Greek word *apostolos* means 'someone who has been sent', a 'messenger'. The Gospel writers sometimes used it to mean messengers in a general sense, e.g. in Luke 11.49 and John 13.16. But more often they used it specifically to mean twelve of Jesus's disciples, whom He sent out to preach (Matt. 10.2; Mark 6.30; Luke 6.13; 17.5; 22.14; 24.10). In the Acts of the Apostles Luke nearly always uses the word only for the Twelve (the twelve Apostles named as such in the Gospels, minus Judas Iscariot, and plus Matthias: Acts 1.2, 26; 2.37, 42, 43, 4.33, etc.); but in Acts 14.4 he also refers to Paul and Barnabas as Apostles. Both in the Acts and in this letter it is stressed that an Apostle must have been appointed by Christ.

Not from men. No other human being, but Jesus Himself had appointed Paul to be an Apostle.

Nor through man. Jesus had appointed Paul directly, without using any go-between.

1.2. And all the brethren who are with me. Paul was not working alone, but in fellowship with the Church, and in close co-operation with some fellow-preachers.

The Churches in Galatia. *Galatai*, 'Galatians', is the Greek name for Celts, and Galatia was called after three Celtic tribes who had settled in the area round Ancyra (present-day Ankara in Turkey) in the third century BC. But the Roman province of Galatia was much larger than the area inhabited by the Galatians themselves, and its southern half was peopled largely by Phrygians, Lycaonians and Pisidians. Scholars are divided on the question whether Paul wrote this letter to Churches in northern Galatia, or to those in southern Galatia mentioned in Acts 13—14, that is to say, Pisidian Antioch, Iconium, Lystra and Derbe. On the one hand, the people in southern Galatia were not actually Galatians, so it may seem strange for Paul to have addressed them by that name (3.1). On the other hand, we do not know that Paul ever visited northern Galatia; some people think that Acts 16.6 refers to northern Galatia, but 'the region of Phrygia and Galatia' probably means the border area between the two provinces, that is to say, the region of Pisidian Antioch. On the whole it seems more likely that this letter was addressed to the Churches mentioned in Acts 13—14. Paul may have thought it easier to call them 'the Churches in Galatia' and their members 'Galatians', rather than use such a clumsy expression as 'O foolish Phrygians, Lycaonians and Pisidians' (3.1).

1.3. Grace to you. Paul used the Greek word *charis*, meaning 'grace', instead of the usual Greek greeting, *chaire*, which means 'be happy'. Greetings often contain such a wish, such as *salute* or *salud*, from the Latin *salve*, which was originally a wish for 'good health'. Paul wanted to wish his readers more than happiness: he wished them God's favour, which does give happiness, but is much more.

And peace. This is a translation of the Jewish greeting, *shalom*. It sounds rather solemn in English, and may have been unusual in Greek, but to Paul it was no more solemn than the equivalent *salaam* or *salama* is in many countries today. However, when Jesus greeted His disciples with 'Peace' (John 20.21, 26), He wanted to say more than 'Good evening', and really did give them His peace. So Paul too wanted to convey the full meaning of God's peace, which is based on the 'security' which comes from being in the right relationship with God and our fellow human beings.

From God the Father and our Lord Jesus Christ. The apostolic greeting does not come from Paul and his companions, but from God. Paul was an Apostle, and therefore a man under orders, like an errand-boy: unimportant in his own right, but authorized to speak and to act in God's name.

1.4. Who gave Himself. Paul stresses that Jesus offered Himself of His own free will (see John 14.30–31: 'the ruler of this world ... has no power over me; but I do as the Father has commanded me').

The present evil age. The biblical writers did not think in terms of the contrast between time and eternity, but of the contrast between the present 'evil' age and the 'age to come', when God will not only *be* King, but *be seen* to be King. The age to come was expected to be in the future; but several New Testament writers stress in various ways that those who belong to Christ have already been delivered from the present evil age. Christians already belong to the age to come. They are citizens of the New Jerusalem (4.26; Phil. 3.20). The Kingdom of God is among them (Luke 17.21), and the City of God is forever 'coming down out of heaven from God' (Rev. 21.2, 10).

'Paul was a man under orders' (p. 5). Like these soldiers on active service in south-east Asia, he had been 'called up' and commissioned by Christ to be an Apostle. How far does serving Christ really resemble serving as a soldier?

INTERPRETATION

Every nation has its own particular way of beginning and ending a letter. The French are probably the shortest in their beginnings: in a formal letter they just write *Monsieur*, 'Sir', or *Madame*, 'Madam', or *Mademoiselle*, 'Miss'; but they end their letters with expressions of flattery and respect. The English write, 'Dear So-and-so', even if they do not know the person to whom they are writing. Arabs begin with a long string of greetings. Iranians apologize for presuming to write at all. In Paul's world it was the custom to begin with the name of the writer, followed by the name of the addressee, and a wish of 'joy' or 'happiness', so the normal beginning of this letter would have been, 'Paul to the Churches in Galatia, joy'. Paul did not alter this pattern, but he did alter the words, for he had more to give than merely a wish for the Galatians' happiness.

Paul also wished to stress first of all that he was an Apostle, duly appointed by God the Father and Jesus Christ as the others had been. Even though Paul had not followed Jesus during His life on earth, Jesus Himself had called him to be an Apostle, and had done so directly. No one else was involved in Paul's apostolate. So he was not a representative of the earlier Apostles, nor their 'successor'; and because he had been appointed and commissioned by Christ, he had the same authority as the other Apostles.

Paul had good reason to state that God raised Jesus Christ from the dead (v. 1): it was the risen Lord Himself who had appeared to him on the road to Damascus (see Acts 9.1–9). So if anyone in the Galatian Churches was questioning his apostolate, they were criticizing what Christ had done to him.

The Churches in Galatia had been founded by Paul. He had worked there, some people had gladly accepted the gospel he brought, and a number of young Churches had come into being. When we read the Acts of the Apostles, it may seem surprising that Paul and his companions seem to have worked in each town for only a short time, appointed some people to lead the congregations, and then left them as young but independent Churches. We should not assume that in most cases all this took only a few weeks, but certainly the foundation of many early Churches took only a few years at the very most.

These young Churches were not left entirely to themselves. There was regular coming and going between the Churches, and between them and the Mother Church in Jerusalem. Considering that all journeys had to be made on foot or on a donkey, or by ship, people in the Roman Empire did an amazing amount of travelling. So the young Churches had the advantage of regular contact with other Churches. Moreover, missionaries kept in touch with the Churches they had founded. Paul's letters show how much he cared for the people to whom he had preached the gospel; and if there were any problems in any of those Churches, he would write to them, or even visit them again. But he seems to have interfered only when it was really necessary. He did regard the members of those Churches as his spiritual 'children', but as grown-up children (see note on 4.19). So Paul allowed them to get on with their Christian lives, and to make their own decisions.

However, events in the Galatian Churches had led to a situation in which Paul could not continue to let them get on with things. These Churches had been visited by other Christian preachers who had caused a great deal of confusion. They seem to have been convinced that they alone knew the whole truth, and they did not approve of Paul's presentation of the gospel. Their preaching probably ran more or less on these lines: 'We know that Paul preached the gospel to you, and you ought to be grateful to him. But it is only fair to tell you that he has not told you the whole truth. For one thing, he does not know the whole truth, for he never followed Jesus when He walked on earth. Moreover, he has no authority to preach the gospel, for he is not an Apostle, and he was not sent by the Apostles. Also, he has tried to make things easy for you, by leaving out some awkward truths, and that is not good enough. Now we will tell you the whole truth. . . .'

This is what made it necessary for Paul, right at the beginning of his letter, to stress that he had been commissioned directly by Christ, without any intermediary.

Paul's greeting to the Galatians was thus more than just a pious wish. As a representative of Christ, he had something to offer. He was in a position, not merely to *wish* them, but to *offer* them 'grace and peace from God the Father and our Lord Jesus Christ'. A person who is commissioned to carry the good news of Christ can speak and act with authority. Paul does not explain this in detail, but the authority implied is the same as that which is described more fully in John 20.23a: 'If you forgive the sins of any, they are forgiven.' The offer, of God's grace in the one case, of the forgiveness of sins in the other, is a genuine offer from God, and can be accepted.

Paul ended his greeting by praising God.

STUDY SUGGESTIONS

WORD STUDY

1. (a) What is the exact meaning of the word 'Apostle'?
   (b) In what two ways was it chiefly used by writers in the NT?
   (c) What are the differences between the words 'Apostle', 'minister'

and 'missionary'? Is it possible to be one without also being the others?

2. (a) What is the meaning of the Hebrew word '*shalom*'?
   (b) In what way do Jews use the word?
   (c) How should we normally translate it into English?
   (d) Why did many of the NT writers translate it literally into Greek, and why do we still do the same into English?

REVIEW OF CONTENT

3. (a) Why is it difficult for us to know precisely where the 'Galatian' Churches were?
   (b) The Roman Province of Galatia was larger than the area actually inhabited by Galatians. What other peoples were among its inhabitants?

4. In what way and for what reason did Paul alter the usual way of beginning a letter in Greek, when he wrote to the Churches?

5. What is the difference in meaning between the two phrases: 'not from men' and 'nor through men'? Why did Paul use both phrases?

6. Why was Paul particularly anxious to establish his authority as an Apostle?

7. What sort of relationships were there between the various young Churches in Paul's time, and what was their relationship with their 'missionaries'?

BIBLE STUDY

8. Read the following passages, and say in each case whether the writer was referring to (i) messengers generally, or (ii) one or other or all of the Twelve Apostles whom Jesus appointed to preach and heal.
   (a) Luke 6.13   (b) Luke 11.49   (c) Acts 1.26   (d) Acts 14.14
   (e) John 13.16   (f) Rev. 2.2   (g) Rev. 21.14

DISCUSSION AND APPLICATION

9. Paul's opening words clearly emphasize the authority of his words for the Galatians. What does this mean for us who read his words today?

10. Some Christian ministers and missionaries today are appointed and authorized by the central organization of the Church or denomination to which they belong; some by the state; and some by the individual congregation which they serve.
    (a) By which method are ministers and missionaries appointed and authorized in your own Church, and what do you see as the advantages and disadvantages compared with other methods?
    (b) How far do you think it is important for a minister to have

such authority? In what circumstances, if any, can a person 'minister' without such authority? Give reasons for your answers.

11. What did Paul mean by the phrase 'the present evil age'? In what way, if any, do you think that the 'present age' is any better or worse today than in Paul's time?

1.6–10

Paul's Reason for Writing

SUMMARY

1.6. Paul was astonished that the Galatians were attracted to a different 'gospel'.

1.7–9. There is no other gospel than that which Paul preached, and which the Galatians had believed.

1.10. Paul was not trying to win anybody's favour.

NOTES

1.6. I am astonished. This is rather different from what Paul usually wrote after his greetings: e.g. 'I thank my God' (Rom. 1.8; Phil. 1.3; Philemon 4), or similar words of thanks (1 Cor. 1.4; 1 Thess. 1.2; 2 Thess. 1.3), or a word of praise to God (2 Cor. 1.3).

Him who called you, that is to say, God. In using the verb 'call', Paul always meant that it is God who calls.

1.6–7. A different gospel—not that there is another gospel, or, 'a different gospel. Not that it is in fact another gospel' (NEB). Paul deliberately distinguished between the two words, 'different' and 'another', to emphasize that what the Galatians were tempted to accept, was not 'another gospel'. It was something entirely different, something that was not a gospel at all.

To pervert, the Greek word means, 'to change into its opposite'. The opposite of good news is bad news.

1.8, 9. Accursed. The Greek word *anathema* means, 'something given to a god' or 'to God'. Outside the Bible this usually means a gift to a Temple in fulfilment of a vow, but the translators of the Old Testament into Greek used it for something, or someone, that had been cast out of the community and left to God's judgement. The REB translates correctly: 'Let him be banned'.

1.10. Still pleasing men. Before his conversion Paul had been 'pleasing' the Jewish authorities by persecuting the Church, but now that he was a servant of Christ he only wanted to please God (see Acts 8.1b–3; 9.1–2). Until recently most English translators used 'men' for the Greek word *anthropoi*; but *anthropoi* means, 'human beings' (NJB), 'people', 'men and women'. In Greek there is another word for men as distinct from women.

INTERPRETATION

Paul usually started his letters, after the initial greeting, with a word of thanks to God for the faith and life of his readers, but in this case he could only express his amazement and alarm at the fickleness of the Galatian Christians. The very strong words which Paul used here show that, in his view at least, the matter was extremely serious.

The preachers who had caused the trouble in Galatia seem to have been convinced that they had the whole truth, and that anyone who disagreed with them was distorting the truth, or not telling the whole truth. So they saw it as their first duty to convert other Christians to their particular sort of Christianity. Their chief aim was, not to convert unbelievers to the Christian faith, but to convert Christians to their particular point of view, and to their way of life.

This sort of thing has always been happening in the Church; it still happens, and it often causes great confusion. People who have put their trust in Jesus, but are not able to put their beliefs into clear words, can be very disturbed if somebody tells them that they are all wrong in their beliefs. It is no secret that Christians differ in their beliefs, and in the ways in which they conduct their worship and their lives. This was already happening in Paul's time. These differences are serious, and we should discuss them, and try to reach an agreement about them. But we also have to accept that we know imperfectly, and only in part (see 1 Cor. 13.9, 12), so maybe we shall continue to differ in our beliefs, our worship, and our ways of life, and must seek to achieve Christian unity in spite of our differences.

However, the belief that one has the whole truth, and that everybody else is wrong, is a great danger to the unity of the Church, and has, in fact, led to deep divisions among Christians. Christians who believed that they alone had the whole truth, have often persecuted other Christians with whom they did not agree. And we have only to think of what has been happening in Northern Ireland, Lebanon, South Africa, and in some Latin American countries in our own time, to recognize that Christians still disagree and persecute other Christians today.

So the activity of these preachers in Galatia was harmful, quite apart from the question of what they actually preached. But the violent words with which Paul attacked his Galatian opponents show that he thought that in this case there was more at stake than a difference of opinion. Paul himself had very precise views on many matters of faith and life; his other letters show that he was used to controversy, and also that he could use fairly strong language to express his views and to counter his opponents. But nowhere else in his writings do we find such fierce language as in this letter. In his view the Galatians had been led astray, not by a different interpretation of the gospel, but by something that was not a gospel at all. His opponents were preaching the very opposite of the gospel, not good news, but bad news, and the Galatians were tempted to accept this bad news! This could only mean that they were beginning to turn away from God. But no one who preaches such bad news must be accepted in the Church. Even if Paul himself, or an angel from heaven, brought a message contrary to the gospel of Jesus Christ, he must be cast out of the Church, and left to God's judgement.

These were strong words, and Paul did not expect the Galatians to like him for writing them. But he was not trying to make himself popular by speaking soft words, and certainly not by misleading them. Nor was he trying to give them what they wanted by telling them what they wished to hear. He was a servant of Christ, so he had to act and speak as his Master told him.

STUDY SUGGESTIONS

WORD STUDY

1. Which *three* of the following words are nearest in meaning to 'pervert' as used in v. 7?
   convert   purvey   distort   revise   deform   misteach   reform
2. (a) What meaning did the translators of the OT into Greek give to the word which is translated as 'accursed' in the RSV (vv. 8–9)?
   (b) Write a short sentence to show its meaning as used by Paul in those verses. (You may find it helpful to look, if you can, at the way the word is translated in other modern versions of the Bible.)

REVIEW OF CONTENT

3. What was the chief aim of the preachers who had been causing the Galatians to disbelieve Paul's teaching?
4. Paul accused the Galatians of 'turning to a different gospel ... contrary to that which we preached to you'. But he also said 'Not that there is another gospel'. If the preaching of Paul's opponents was not 'another gospel', what was it?

5. 'If I were still pleasing men, I should not be a servant of Christ' (v. 10).
   (a) Who were the 'men' Paul had previously been trying to please?
   (b) How had he tried to please them?
   (c) Why was he no longer pleasing them?

BIBLE STUDY

6. (a) What is the chief difference between what Paul wrote after his greeting to the Galatians (v. 6), and what he usually wrote after his greetings in letters to other Churches, e.g. in Rom. 1.8; 1 Cor. 1.4; Phil. 1.3; 1 Thess. 1.2; 2 Thess. 1.3?
   (b) How would a present-day preacher or teacher be likely to start a letter to a congregation he had visited?

DISCUSSION AND APPLICATION

7. Describe what happens when Christians who believe that they alone have the whole truth try to convert other Christians to their ideas and way of life? How is such preaching likely to affect (a) individual Christians, and (b) congregations or other groups of Christians?
8. Paul said that the Galatians should treat as 'accursed' anyone whose preaching was 'contrary' to what he had taught them. Today there are deep divisions between the Churches, but some Christians say 'We all preach the same gospel; disagreements over religion are a waste of time, we should live and let live.' How far do you agree with this view? Give your reasons.
9. The world-famous scientist Albert Einstein wrote: 'Great spirits have encountered violent opposition from mediocre minds' (and a certain Christian minister sometimes wears a t-shirt with this statement written on the front!). How far do you think the statement applies in the case of Paul's opponents?

1.11–24

How Paul became an Apostle

SUMMARY

1.11–12. Paul received the gospel from Christ Himself.

1.13–14. Paul's past as a zealous Jew.

1.15–17. When he was called to preach Christ to the Gentiles, he did not confer with those who were Christians before him.

1.18–20. He did not meet Peter and James until three years later, and had not met any of the other Jerusalem Apostles.

1.21–24. When he worked in Syria and Cilicia, he was still unknown to the Churches in Judea; but they heard of his work, and praised God for it.

NOTES

1.11. Brethren. This is a rather old-fashioned word for 'brothers'. But the Greek word which it is used to translate can also mean 'brothers and sisters'. So except in cases where it is clearly addressed to men only, we should translate 'brothers and sisters'.

Not man's gospel, or 'not according to man' (RSV, margin). This could mean (a) 'not a human invention' (NEB); or (b) 'not something that suits the taste of human beings' (see 1 Cor. 2.9); or (c) 'not something that I learned from any human being'. Perhaps Paul wanted to convey all three meanings.

1.12. It came through a revelation. That is, through a *direct* revelation in which Jesus Himself showed Paul the truth of the gospel: no other human being was involved in it (see Acts 9.3–6).

1.13. I persecuted the Church of God violently. This accords with the picture given by Luke, e.g. in Acts 9.1.

1.14. Advanced in Judaism. See Acts 22.3.

1.16. Flesh and blood was a common Jewish expression for 'human beings'.

1.18. After three years. Biblical references to time are difficult to interpret, because in those days people counted inclusively, that is to say, they included both the beginning and the end. For example, any period that started in the year 800 of the Roman calendar, and ended in the year 802, would be called 'three years'; so this could mean the 366 days from 31 December 800 till 1 January 802, or the 1094 days from 1 January 800 till 31 December 802, or anything in between. Paul's information therefore does not give us precise dates for these events.

Cephas, that is, Simon Peter. In Aramaic (the everyday language of Palestine at that time) *keifa* means a 'rock'; this was the new name which Jesus gave to Simon (John 1.42). Most NT writers translated the name into Greek as *Petros*, but Paul usually called him 'Cephas' (except in 2.7).

1.19. James the Lord's brother. This James had not been a disciple during Jesus's ministry (see Mark 6.3; Matt. 13.55), but became a disciple after His resurrection (1 Cor. 15.7), and soon became a leading figure in the Jerusalem Church (2.9; Acts 12.17). When Peter left Jerusalem, James became the leader of the Church there (Acts 15.13; 21.18).

1.21. The regions of Syria and Cilicia. This covers a wide area, including both Tarsus and Antioch (see Acts 11.25–26).

INTERPRETATION

Paul's purpose in writing this section was to give evidence for the claim he had made in v. 1, that Christ Himself had made him an Apostle. So he did not give a detailed account of his conversion such as we find in the Acts of the Apostles (Acts 9.1–19; 22.3–16; 26.9–18). Instead he stressed that both his conversion and his call to the ministry were due to God's grace. It was not his choice, but God's choice that he should be an Apostle to the Gentiles.

How much this was God's work, is shown by the fact that Paul had been a good Jew, and more zealous than most in his hostility to the Church. However, his words also had another purpose. His opponents insisted on the Jewishness of the Christian faith, and the importance of certain commandments of the Jewish Law. Paul could beat them at their own game. He was himself a Jew, brought up in the Jewish faith, and he knew more about the Jewish Law than his opponents. Paul had not chosen to become a Christian and an Apostle: God had chosen him, even before he was born (v. 15). We must not exaggerate this, as if Paul had no decision to make at all: he had to *respond* to God's calling. But the deciding factor was God's decision (see also John 15.16). And Paul had received the gospel directly from Christ through a revelation, not through any human being.

When Paul wrote, 'I did not confer with flesh and blood' (v. 16), he did not mean that he never spoke to any other Christians about the Christian faith. Of course he did. But he did not have to ask them to confirm his authority as an Apostle, for this was something Christ had already given him, with a special commission to the Gentiles.

So he did not hurry to meet the other Apostles after his conversion. He did not go up to Jerusalem until some years later, when he met Peter and John. No doubt these three had much to say to each other, but Peter and James did not have to provide Paul with his apostolic authority, for he had that already. His case was different from that of Matthias (Acts 1.15–26), who had been chosen through the means of a meeting of the disciples. Paul had not even met any of the other Apostles.

So the Church in Jerusalem had neither called Paul, nor ordained him. All that the Churches in Judea could do, was to take note of what God had done, to appreciate that he was now preaching the faith that he had previously tried to destroy, and to praise God because of him. And that is what they did do.

STUDY SUGGESTIONS

WORD STUDY

1. In English, 'brethren' is an old-fashioned word meaning 'brothers'. What can the Greek word translated as 'brethren' in v. 11 also mean, and how should it be translated today?
2. What does the Jewish expression 'flesh and blood' mean in v. 16?

REVIEW OF CONTENT

3. (a) What was Paul's chief purpose in writing this passage?
   (b) What did he write in order to achieve that purpose?
4. Why did Paul remind the Galatians that he had been 'advanced in Judaism' and 'extremely zealous' for Jewish traditions (v. 14)?
5. Why did Paul emphasize:
   (a) that after his conversion he 'went away into Arabia'?
   (b) that he did not meet any of the other Apostles until three years later, and then only Peter and James?
   (c) that the Churches in Judaea had 'glorified God' because of him?

BIBLE STUDY

6. Read Acts 9.1–22, and then say:
   (a) How did Paul know that what had happened to him on the road to Damascus was 'a revelation of Jesus Christ' (v. 12)?
   (b) What was the 'gospel' which came to Paul through that revelation?
7. Compare Gal. 1.15–24 with Acts 9.19b–31. How do you account for the differences between the two descriptions of Paul's activity following his conversion? How important do you consider those differences? Give your reasons.

DISCUSSION AND APPLICATION

8. (a) Do you think that Paul was chiefly concerned to defend his own authority as a person against the accusations of his opponents, or the authority of the gospel he preached, as opposed to their preaching? Give reasons for your answer.
   (b) What would be your own reaction if someone questioned your 'authority' to speak of the gospel as you do?
9. How would you answer someone who asked the following question?
   'Paul was not one of the Twelve, he had never met Jesus, and he was not present at Pentecost, so how could he claim to be a true Apostle?'
10. Some ministries in the Church today are described as 'apostolic'.

Give examples, and say what you think the term 'apostolic' means in the context of the present-day Church.
11. What is implied in the word 'revelation' as used by Paul in v. 15? How can we distinguish between a revelation sent by God, and the sort of 'dreams' and fantasies we sometimes have about ourselves, and which are really 'self-delusion'?

Special Note A
Grace

The gospel is the message of God's grace. This is therefore an important word in the Christian vocabulary, and much has been said and written about it. But if we want to understand what Paul meant by 'grace', we must turn to the Old Testament, where 'grace' is expressed chiefly by two Hebrew words.

The first of these, *hen*, is translated in various ways, but the phrase 'to find favour in someone's sight' shows its meaning most clearly. This phrase was used in petitioning a ruler or overseer to grant some request, as when Joab was grateful that he had 'found favour' in King David's sight (2 Sam. 14.22; see also Esth. 8.5). 'Grace and favour' meant the ruler's kindness to his subjects, and shows that the gracious ruler and the ordinary people existed on very different levels. The expression was not confined to the court: Ruth hoped to find favour in Boaz's sight (Ruth 2.2); but it always assumed inequality between the person who asked and the person who received the favour. It was not given automatically, but required an act of condescension.

Some people today regard such subservience on one side and condescension on the other as 'paternalism', and argue for or against it. However, in the ancient world these inequalities were taken very seriously, and we could point to many situations in the modern world where all the power is on one side, and people hope for 'favour' from 'top management', or the boss or foreman, in business or industrial enterprises. And whatever we think about inequalities between humans, there can be no doubt about the absolute distinction between God and us. True, He created us, but this does not mean that we can demand His favour as of right. We are not only very insignificant, but we are also sinners, who have offended Him. The amazing thing about God's grace is that He should know and love and be concerned about us at all.

Besides this condescension, there is also an element of kindly humour in the word '*hen*'. In Amsterdam, where the local speech contains many Hebrew words, many people use the word only for that sense of

In the Old Testament 'grace and favour' required 'an act of condescension' (p. 17). We can see a reflection of this in the inequality between the Fijian government minister who comes from a line of Chiefs, and his secretary taking dictation. But the amazing thing about *God's* grace is that He loves and cares for us at all.

humour which enables them to smile at their own troubles. It suggests that people who take God seriously should beware of being too serious about themselves. We should not actually translate '*hen*' by the word 'humour', but in this sense it reminds us that God bestows His grace with a smile, and that those who enjoy His favour can see themselves in a sunny light. So when Abraham 'found favour' with God, and Sarah at last bore him a son, they very properly called the boy 'Isaac', meaning 'God smiles' (Gen. 17.19–20; 18.1–5).

The second word is *hesed*, which the AV translates by 'mercy' or '(loving) kindness', and the RSV usually (but not always) by 'steadfast love'. *Hesed* means a loyalty, love and kindness, which is undeserved, and which remains constant and steadfast, whatever happens. When it is used of human beings, it often means an act of kindness which we might not have expected, or a good deed which most people would not regard as a duty. God wants people to practise *hesed* (Micah 6.8). The action of the Good Samaritan was an act of mercy (Luke 10.37).

The word *hesed* contains an element of surprise, and when it is used of God, it stresses that His mercy is *amazing* grace. God does not owe us anything; moreover, we have offended against His love, and keep on offending Him. Yet He continues to care for us and surround us with His love. In the Psalms the singers never cease to be amazed at God's steadfast love.

The two words *hen* and *hesed* are never used as if they meant exactly the same, but they both emphasize that God's unfailing goodness is not something He owes us: He grants us his grace entirely of His own free will.

The Greek word *charis*, which Paul used for the grace of God, means 'that which pleases', but in New Testament times it was used for the 'favour' granted by a ruler to his subjects. Like *hesed*, it emphasizes that God's kindness is undeserved and unexpected. In 1.15 Paul makes it clear that he had not deserved his calling to be an Apostle, and in Romans 3.24 he stressed that God's goodness is not a reward for what people have done. The Church later expressed this in Latin by the phrase '*gratia gratis data*', 'grace freely given'.

However, God's grace is not merely one of His attributes: it is God Himself making His undeserved and unfailing love known to His people, a love that springs entirely from Him.

STUDY SUGGESTIONS

WORD STUDY

1. What two Hebrew words for 'grace' would Paul have had in mind

when writing this letter? What was the exact meaning of each, and what meaning did they have in common?

2. Which *five* of the following words would you use in describing God's grace?

mercy elegance favour beauty adornment loving-kindness style charm condescension forgiveness partiality

What other English words or phrases can you think of, which relate to God's grace as described in this section?

REVIEW OF CONTENT

3. (a) What aspect of God's grace was Paul particularly concerned to emphasize? Give examples to support your answer.

(b) For what reason did Paul wish to emphasize that aspect of God's grace?

BIBLE STUDY

4. What do we learn about God's grace from each of the following passages?

(a) Ps. 103.6–14 (b) Jonah 4.2 (c) Rom. 5.1–8 (d) Gal. 5.4–6
(e) Eph. 2.4–10 (f) 2 Thess. 2.16 (g) Heb. 12.14–15

DISCUSSION AND APPLICATION

5. In what chief way have all Christians received God's grace, and in what ways do we continue to receive His grace? In what particular ways, if any, do you feel that you have yourself experienced God's grace?

6. G. K. Chesterton wrote: 'There was some one thing that was too great for God to show us when He walked upon earth, and I have sometimes fancied that it was his mirth.' If 'there is an element of kindly humour' in God's dealing with us (pp. 17–18), do you think Chesterton was right in what he wrote? If not, in what ways does God show His humour in His relationship with human beings?

7. If there is an element of kindly humour in God's dealing with us, how should that affect our attitude to our own beliefs and actions? Should we be able to laugh at our own actions and even at some of our beliefs? Give your reasons.

8. Paul claimed that he had been set apart and called to be an Apostle through God's grace (l. 15). How far, if at all, do you think anyone can be an effective minister of the gospel *without* God's grace?

Paul's Agreement with the Jerusalem Apostles

SUMMARY

2.1–2. After several years Paul visited Jerusalem to come to an agreement with the leaders there about his work.

2.3–5. Titus, a Gentile Christian who was with him, was not compelled to be circumcised.

2.6–10. James, Peter and John acknowledged that Paul had been called to be an Apostle to the Gentiles, and arranged with him a division of the missionary work.

NOTES

2.1. After fourteen years. This is not a precise figure, see note on l. 18; moreover, Paul does not say whether he is reckoning from his conversion or from his return to Syria and Cilicia.

Barnabas was a Cypriot Jew, who had joined the Church in Jerusalem, where he became noted for his generosity (Acts 4.36–37). According to Luke he introduced Paul to the earlier Apostles (Acts 9.27). Later the Jerusalem Church sent him to Antioch in Syria, to see what was happening in the Church there, where so many members were Gentile Christians (Acts 11.19–26). He seems to have approved of what he found there (2.13). While at Antioch, he sent for Paul (Acts 11.25), and afterwards he went with Paul and John Mark on a mission to his native land of Cyprus (Acts 13.1–12). He also accompanied Paul during the mission to southern Galatia (Acts 13.13—14.28), but they quarrelled over whether John Mark should continue to accompany them, and parted before their next missionary journeys (Acts 15.36–40). However, they seem to have made up and worked together again later (see 1 Cor. 9.6; Philemon 24).

Titus was probably known to Paul's readers. He is not mentioned in the Acts of the Apostles, and scholars differ as to whether this was the Titus to whom the Letter of that name was addressed.

2.2. Privately. There was no meeting with the Church as a body.

Lest somehow I should be running or had run in vain. Paul had received his commission from Christ Himself, so he did not need anybody's approval. But he wanted to come to an arrangement with the other Apostles, so that they would not be in each other's way, or hinder each other's work.

2.3. Titus ... though he was a Greek. Paul actually wrote, 'Titus ... being a Greek' (AV), which could mean either 'though ...' or 'because he was a Greek'. 'A Greek' here means a Gentile, i.e. anyone who is not a Jew.

Was not compelled to be circumcised. Many people think that this shows that Paul could not have urged Timothy to be circumcised as stated in Acts 16.3. But the two cases were different. Timothy's mother was a Jewess, so he was already a Jew (according to the rabbis everyone born from a Jewish mother is a Jew, no matter who the father is). The circumcision of Timothy would have shown that a Jew who became a Christian still remained a Jew. But Titus was not a Jew, and did not have to become one in order to be a Christian.

2.4. But because of ... This sentence does not run very well in Greek, and is awkward in English. The REB translation shows more clearly what Paul meant: 'That course was urged only as a concession to certain sham Christians, intruders who had sneaked in to spy on the liberty we enjoy in the fellowship of Christ Jesus' (REB). It seems that the Jewish authorities had planted some spies in the Church, in order to find out what was happening there, a method still used by some oppressive governments.

That they might bring us into bondage. Paul was implying that to make Gentile Christians keep the letter of the Jewish Law would be the same as making slaves of them, instead of setting them free.

2.6. God shows no partiality. Paul meant that the grace which God had shown to the other Apostles was no greater than the grace He had shown to Paul himself.

2.9. Pillars, that is, people in responsible and important positions who are honoured and respected by their fellows.

The right hand of fellowship is a pledge of friendship. This custom existed among both Jews and Greeks, just as it still does in many countries today.

2.10. To remember the poor. The Church in Jerusalem had many poor members, and needed the support of wealthier Christians (see Acts 11.29; 2 Cor. 8—9).

INTERPRETATION

Having established that Jesus Himself had called him to be an Apostle, Paul now makes it clear that the other Apostles had accepted him as their equal, and had agreed with him on the way in which he conducted his ministry. In a private discussion with the leading Apostles, James, Peter and John, it had been agreed:

1. That Titus need not be circumcised. This was a far-reaching decision, for it meant that Gentiles who became Christians remained Gentiles. This implied that they were not expected to observe the Law of Moses. In this the Apostles simply followed the views of the rabbis: the Law was God's special gift to Israel. Gentiles also ought to do God's will, but God's will for them was expressed in the commandments given to Noah (Gen. 9.4–7). (People who live near Jews today may notice that Jews often ask Gentile friends or neighbours to do things for them which they themselves are not allowed to do, such as, for instance, switching the lights on for them on the sabbath, when in Jewish eyes it is a sin for a Jew to do such things, but not for a Gentile.)

2. That Paul and the others would each work in their own mission field, and they would not interfere with each other. Peter and his friends would work among Jewish communities, and Paul and his companions would work in Gentile territories; and each would be free to follow his own practice.

3. That the fellowship between the various Churches would be maintained, and the Gentile Churches should give support to the poor in Jerusalem.

There is some question as to the precise occasion when Paul reached this agreement with the Jerusalem Apostles. Many scholars believe that Paul is here referring to the meeting recorded in Acts 15. There are great differences between the two accounts, but neither Paul nor Luke was giving a detailed account, and Luke allowed himself considerable freedom when writing the Acts. If the two accounts refer to the same event, we must accept that Paul's is the more accurate.

The chief reason for thinking that Paul and Luke *are* referring to the same meeting is that the decisions made are the same. All that Luke has done was to explain the implications.

But there are also reasons for thinking that Paul may *not* be referring to the same meeting as Luke. The participants are not the same. According to Paul, he and Barnabas and Titus met James, Peter and John privately. Peter was clearly still in Jerusalem. But in Luke's account Peter had already left Jerusalem (Acts 12.19), and only came to support Paul and his helpers. Moreover, the decisions were taken by the whole Church, not by the leaders only at a private meeting.

Though we must allow for the possibility that, when Luke wrote, some of the details may not have been remembered accurately, we must also point out that Luke mentions an earlier visit by Paul and Barnabas to Jerusalem (Acts 11.30; 12.25). He does not say much about this visit, but he does mention that they brought John Mark with them (Acts 12.25), who shortly afterwards accompanied them on their mission to

'The other Apostles had accepted Paul and agreed about the way he conducted his ministry' (pp. 22–23). And just as people do in many situations today—for example when international finance was agreed for development projects in Tanzania—they had shaken hands to confirm the agreement. What is the chief of significance of shaking hands in such situations?

Cyprus (Acts 13.1–12). It seems reasonable to assume that they brought him for that very purpose, and if that is so, it would have been very strange if they had not discussed their plans with the other Apostles. This visit seems to have been the ideal opportunity for seeking the sort of agreement mentioned in Galatians 2.1–10.

However, we must not overrate the importance of such questions, nor forget the chief points which Paul wanted to make:

(a) It was important for the Galatians to know that the Jerusalem Apostles had accepted that Christ Himself had called Paul, who was thus their equal in the sight of God, because that refuted his opponents' attacks on his authority.

(b) It was equally important that the Apostles had agreed that a Gentile Christian was not a Jew, for that counteracted the claim that Christians must obey the Jewish Law, or at least such commandments as Paul's opponents thought necessary. His opponents were acting against the policy of the Mother Church in Jerusalem, and, worse, against the will of Christ.

The agreement clearly left some important questions unanswered. The Christian life must be lived within the community of the Church, and this cannot very well be done without some rules. So the Church did gradually adopt some rules for the conduct of the members' lives, for the conduct of its worship, and for its organization. Some of these rules were derived from the Law of Moses, such as the Ten Commandments (Exod. 20.2–17); some from the teaching of Jesus, such as practices about marriage and divorce (Mark 10.11–12; Matt. 5.31–32); others again from the practice of the Apostles, such as the way in which to celebrate the Eucharist (1 Cor. 11.23–26). Differences between the Churches about the way in which they do these things, arise very often from different interpretations of what we read in the Bible.

Paul was soon to discover that the agreement could be interpreted in more than one way. This also led him to concern himself with a much deeper question: what actually is the validity of law?

STUDY SUGGESTIONS

WORD STUDY

1. In the NT a 'Greek' does not necessarily mean someone belonging to the Greek Nation. What else can it mean?
2. What did Paul mean by the word 'bondage' in 2.4?

REVIEW OF CONTENT

3. Although Paul's authority was not dependent on the Jerusalem

Apostles, he did want to come to an agreement with them. Why did
he think this necessary?

4. (a) For what reasons do some scholars think that Gal. 2.1–10
refers to the same meeting as that described in Acts 15?
(b) For what reasons do others believe that it refers to an earlier
meeting?

5. How does Jewish teaching distinguish between those who are Jews
and those who are not?

6. The Jewish rabbis taught that the Law of Moses was binding on all
Jews. How far did they regard it as binding also on Gentiles?

7. Briefly summarize the agreement reached at the meeting of Paul
with the leading Apostles in Jerusalem, as regards:
(a) the validity of the Jewish Law for Gentiles, and
(b) the division of missionary work as between Paul and Barnabas
on the one hand, and Peter and the other Apostles on the other
hand.

BIBLE STUDY

8. What is the connection between Gal. 2.10 and Acts 11.29, 1 Cor.
16.1–4; and 2 Cor. 8—9?

DISCUSSION AND APPLICATION

9. Get one or two friends to join you in writing a brief description of
some event you have attended together. Then read out the accounts, and note the differences between them. What light do those
differences throw on the differences between Luke's and Paul's
accounts of the Jerusalem meeting (if indeed the two accounts refer
to the same meeting, see p. 23).

10. 'Paul wanted to come to an agreement with the other Apostles'
(p. 22). Find out some of the ways in which Churches and Christian
groups in your country 'come to an agreement' when there are
differences either within or between them. In what circumstances
do they give each other 'the right hand of friendship'?

11. 'False brethren secretly brought in . . . that they might bring us into
bondage' (v. 4). Imagine that you are one of Paul's opponents, and
write a letter to tell the Galatians why you believe Paul's teaching
was wrong, and what you think they should think and do instead.

2.11–21
A Conflict between Peter and Paul

SUMMARY

2.11–12a. At Antioch Jewish and Gentile Christians often had meals together, and when Peter came to Antioch, he joined in.

2.12b–13. But when some people from Jerusalem arrived, and objected to the practice, Peter and other Jewish Christians withdrew from these meals.

2.14–21. Paul rebuked Peter, asking him how he, a Jew who lived like a Gentile, could force Gentiles to live like Jews. He pointed out that both Jews and Gentiles are justified, not by works of the law, but through faith in Jesus Christ.

NOTES

2.11. Antioch in Syria (now Antakya in southern Turkey), one of the largest cities of the Roman Empire, had a large Jewish community, and became an important centre of the Christian Church (Acts 11.19–26). It must not be confused with other cities of the same name, such as Pisidian Antioch (Acts 13.14).

2.12. From James. See note on 1.19. James, who strictly obeyed the Mosaic Law, was now the leader of the Church in Jerusalem.

Ate with the Gentiles. Meals were a problem because food provided by Gentiles would not have been prepared according to the strict rules laid down in the Mosaic Law for *kosher* ('clean') food. It might even include such forbidden meats as pork, so Jews were, and are, not allowed to touch it, just as Muslims must only eat *halal* food, and Hindus are not allowed to eat beef. The strictest Jews went even further, and believed that all contact with Gentiles was defiling.

The circumcision party. Paul actually wrote, 'those of the circumcision' (see AV). 'The circumcision' means 'the Jews' (as it does in 2.7, 8, 9; Rom. 3.30). The REB translates correctly, 'because he was afraid of the Jews'.

2.14. They were not straightforward. Most English translators interpret Paul's Greek expression, *ouk orthopodousin*, as meaning, 'not walking in a straight line'. As no Greek writer had used the word before, it is difficult to know what it means. *Orthopous* means 'standing upright', so Paul may have meant that they were not walking upright

27

(see AV, RV), but limping, and this makes more sense. They were limping on two unequal ideas (see 1 Kings 18.21), like a cripple who has to walk on two unequal legs.

2.15. Not Gentile sinners. This seems to imply that Peter and Paul continued to observe the Mosaic Law in as far as this did not interfere with the Christian fellowship. Paul was not opposed to the Law, but to what he regarded as a wrong use of the Law.

2.16. Is not justified, see Special Note C.

By works ... through faith. Paul used two different prepositions: *by* works, *through* faith. *By* refers to the cause: those who believe that they are justified *by* works of law, think that their deeds make them acceptable to God. *Through* refers to the means: those who believe that they are justified *through* faith, believe that God has already accepted them: their faith is the means by which they receive the gift: 'for by grace you have been saved, through faith; and this is not your doing, it is the gift of God' (Eph. 2.8). The Letter to the Ephesians may or may not be by Paul, but this verse expresses his message admirably. However, Paul was not always so careful with his use of 'by' and 'through' (see the second half of v. 16, and also v. 21).

Faith in Jesus Christ. The Greek could also be translated, 'the faithfulness of Jesus Christ', see Special Note B.

2.17. In our endeavour to be justified. A better translation of what Paul wrote is, 'in seeking to be justified' (NEB, REB, NIV).

We ourselves were found to be sinners. In order to maintain the Christian fellowship, Peter and Paul had transgressed against the Mosaic Law, so according to the letter of the Law they had become 'sinners'.

2.18. Those things which I tore down. This could mean either (a) those provisions of the Law which interfered with the Christian fellowship, and which Paul no longer observed, or (b) the belief that obedience to the Law justifies a person before God, a belief that he no longer held; or it could mean both.

Then I prove myself a transgressor. This is not clear. It could mean (a) 'Then I prove that my conduct had been wrong', that is to say, if Paul (or Peter) returned to a strict obedience to the letter of the Law, he would show that it had been wrong for him to have given up his strict obedience at first. Or it could mean (b) 'Then I would be really sinning', that is to say, returning to a strict obedience to the letter of the Law would be the real sin. This seems more likely to be what Paul meant.

2.21. Justification. Paul wrote 'righteousness' (NIV, REB): Paul is not simply repeating that the Law does not justify us, but goes further: obedience to the Law does not make us righteous (see 3.9).

Then Christ died to no purpose. If the Mosaic Law was the gateway to God, then the death of Christ would not have served any purpose. But, as Paul was to argue later (3.6–18), the Law never was the gateway to God.

INTERPRETATION

Paul continues his letter by describing a conflict between Peter and himself, which had taken place at Antioch in Syria some time after the agreement mentioned in vv. 1–10. Paul told the Galatians about this for three reasons, (1) to show once more that he was not a mere follower of the earlier Apostles; (2) to illustrate how interference in the life of a Church is likely to break up the Christian fellowship; and (3) to lay a foundation for his argument against his opponents.

Antioch was probably the first Church in which there were both Jews and Gentiles in significant numbers, and it had become the custom for Jews and Gentiles 'to eat together'. We do not know whether Paul means (a) that they celebrated the Lord's Supper together, which would have been the natural thing to do anyway, or whether he meant (b) that they also joined in a common meal of the congregation, the *agape* or 'love-meal', which was, and is practised in some Churches, or (c) that they shared meals in each other's houses. For the interpretation of this passage it makes no difference, for in any case there would be problems about the Jewish food laws. The practice probably developed quite naturally out of the Christian fellowship, without much conscious thought. It was really unthinkable to have separate Communion services for different sets of people; and when people are close to each other, they will also have meals together.

When Peter arrived at Antioch, it probably did not occur to him to act differently from the other Christians there, so he did the same. But afterwards some visitors arrived from Jerusalem, evidently sent by James, in order to see what was happening at Antioch; and they were horrified at seeing fellow Jewish Christians sharing meals with Gentiles. Not only did they refuse to join in, but they persuaded the local Jewish Christians to abandon the practice. Paul's words, 'because he was afraid of the Jews' (see note on v. 12) suggest that the visitors had pointed out that, by having meals with Gentiles, they were breaking their ties with their fellow-Jews, and particularly with the Jewish Christian Church in Jerusalem.

These visitors do not seem to have been a 'circumcision party', for they did not demand that the Gentile Christians should be circumcised, nor that these Gentiles should observe the food laws. All that they asked was that the Jewish Christians should obey the Law of Moses.

The situation was different from our situation today, because the Church had not yet become divided into a number of different

'Churches'. They were not faced, as we are, with problems about the differences between Churches governed by 'bishops' and those with a 'presbyterial' form of government, or between Churches with an ordained ministry and those with no ordained people. They did not belong to 'another denomination', but were members of a sister Church which had different customs and applied different rules. They felt the same sort of surprise that is felt by people from Churches where the congregation participate in the services actively, and sometimes exuberantly, by spontaneous shouts of joy and hand-clapping, when they attend a service in a Church where the congregation remains quiet. Only in this case the matter was more serious, because the visitors believed that what the people at Antioch did was positively wrong. So instead of regarding the different way things were done at Antioch as an interesting and even enriching experience, they looked upon it with horror, and advised their fellow Jewish Christians to change their ways.

This problem had not been foreseen in the agreement between Paul and the Jerusalem Apostles. That had dealt with different practices in various Churches, on the assumption that each Church would be either Jewish or Gentile. A Jewish Christian Church in Jerusalem could live happily in harmony with a Gentile Church in Caesarea, without being worried about the differences between them. Here the differences existed within the same Church, and Paul saw clearly what other people did not see, that the demands of the visitors would split the Church. If Jewish and Gentile Christians each followed their different customs, then they would become segregated; the Gentile Christians would then soon be regarded as second class Christians; and the only way out of the problem would have been for them to become Jews by circumcision.

Paul had been particularly upset because Peter and Barnabas gave in to the visitors. These two were leading figures in the Church, and their example counted for much. Moreover, they did not give in because they thought the visitors were right, but because they were afraid of what the visitors and the people in Jerusalem might say. No wonder Paul accused them of hypocrisy!

We cannot be sure where Paul's account of his rebuke to Peter ends and his argument with the Galatians begins: much of vv. 15–21 could be directed either at Peter or at the Galatians. Many interpreters regard this passage as evidence that Peter and Paul were habitual opponents, who preached very different gospels. There were certainly differences among the early Christians, and Peter and Paul did probably present the gospel in very different forms (see p. 1). But we have no evidence that they were enemies, or that they headed two parties in the early Church. In this case Paul was not attacking Peter on a matter of principle: Peter had already been living by the principle that Paul advocated. Paul did not have to tell Peter to change his mind: he was urging him to act according to his beliefs.

Paul now comes to the heart of the matter. We are not justified 'by works of the law'. He meant the Law of Moses: even if a person is a good Jew, who knows the Law and keeps it, that does not justify him before God: it cannot make him acceptable to God, if God has not already accepted him. The good news is that God *has* accepted him.

However, Paul's words apply to any law, whether God-given or man-made. All communities have their laws, and every Church has its laws by which its affairs are conducted, and by which its members live. Such rules are necessary, and we should abide by them. But the visitors from Jerusalem made two mistakes, which Peter and Barnabas ought to have recognized. They regarded the ways of the Church in Jerusalem as the only valid ones, at least for Jewish Christians; and they seemed to believe that obeying those rules, which were 'divine laws', justified them before God. But laws are made for people; people are not made for the laws (see Mark 2.27). 'The law is holy, and the commandment is holy and just and good' (Rom. 7.12), and God gave it for a purpose (3.19), but its purpose is not to put us right with God. What justifies us before God is His grace (v. 21); this is God's free gift, and we can receive the gift only if we accept it through faith (v. 16; see Special Note B).

But some people would say that if Jewish Christians disobey the Mosaic food laws, they disobey a divine law, and become 'sinners'. Surely, this means that Christ encourages them to sin, which makes Him an 'agent of sin' (v. 17). Paul's answer is an emphatic, 'certainly not'. He does not argue the case. His idea may have been that the more important command cancels a lesser one. This was a common rabbinic argument. In this case the will of Christ, that His people should be one body (1 Cor. 12.12–13), cancels any less important command.

When Paul was younger he had regarded the Law as a means of getting himself accepted by God. But that was a wrong use of the Law, and he had abandoned it. It would be a grave sin to return to it. He had 'died to the Law'. So the Law no longer had any power over him, for the person who had been governed by the Law was no longer there. Now that he has been baptized, he is a new person (Rom. 6.3–4). His past is dead and buried. He has been 'crucified with Christ', and raised to a radically new life.

This new life does not belong to Paul but to Christ. In it Paul's own achievements are of no importance, for it is Christ who lives in him. There is no room for any attempts of his own to make himself good and righteous, and so to justify himself. Indeed, such an attempt would be impossible, unnecessary and ungodly. Impossible because God owes no one anything, and no one can put God in his debt; unnecessary because

God has already accepted us, and ungodly because it would be ungrateful not to accept what Christ has done for us.

STUDY SUGGESTIONS

WORD STUDY

1. What is the difference in meaning between the words 'by' and 'through' in 'not . . . by works . . . but through faith' (v. 16), and 'by grace you have been saved through faith' (Eph. 2.8)?

REVIEW OF CONTENT

2. For what three reasons did Paul write this passage?
3. (a) What did the visitors from Jerusalem say to the people in Antioch? What did they *not* demand?
   (b) Were the visitors really a 'circumcision party'? Give reasons for your answer.
   (c) What risk did the Antioch Christians run, if they listened to the visitors?
4. How was it possible for the difference in teaching to arise in spite of Paul's earlier agreement with the Jerusalem Apostles?
5. What had Peter's attitude been before the visitors arrived, and how did their arrival affect him?
6. 'The visitors from Jerusalem made two mistakes' (p. 31). What were those mistakes?
7. (a) What did Paul mean when he said that works of law do not justify us before God?
   (b) What did he mean when he said that if justification were through the Law, then Christ 'died to no purpose'?
8. What is one possible interpretation of what Paul meant when he said that if he were to build up again what he had torn down, he would be a 'transgressor'?
9. In what way did Peter and Paul agree, and in what way did they not agree?

BIBLE STUDY

10. What connection, if any, is to be found between the prophet Elijah's words to the Israelites in 1 Kings 18.21 and the words of Paul in Gal. 2.11–16? What do the words imply in each case?
11. What connection is there between Gal. 2.12; Mark 14.66–72; and Acts 4.5–13? What do these three passages tell us about Peter's character?

DISCUSSION AND APPLICATION

12. 'Paul saw ... that the demands of the visitors would split the Church ... Gentiles would be regarded as second class Christians' (p. 30). What are some of the differences which split the Church today? Do any Christians in your country or in your Church regard others as 'second class Christians'? If so, for what reasons?
13. 'It was really unthinkable to have different Communion Services for different people' (p. 29). But today some Churches ban members of some other Churches from participating in Holy Communion with them. Do you think this is right? Give your reasons.
14. 'Paul was not attacking Peter: he was urging him to act according to his beliefs' (pp. 30–31). Some people suggest that in the dispute between Paul and his opponents, Peter was trying to keep the peace by walking a middle path. How can we decide when it is right to compromise in a dispute? What do Paul's words in Gal. 1.10 teach us on the subject?
15. In this passage we see only Paul's side of his disagreement with Peter. What do you think Peter might have said in answer to Paul's accusations?

Special Note B
'Faith' according to Paul

Everyone who has read the New Testament must be aware that 'faith' is one of its key words; and Christians have thought and written much about faith, and examined it from every possible angle. But the New Testament writers and their readers knew the word 'faith' only as it was used in ordinary everyday language; they did not make the distinction between the way in which we speak about 'faith' in a religious sense, and the way in which we use the word when we are not talking about our Christian faith.

The most striking difference is that when we discuss faith in a religious sense, we are usually talking about *our* faith, so we are really talking about ourselves; but when we refer to faith in a secular sense, we are talking first and foremost about someone else. When I say, 'I have faith in so-and-so', I do not mean to say that I have some quality called 'faith', but that the other person is someone whom I can trust. If a man says he has faith in his wife, he means that she can be trusted. And if we say we have faith in someone who has to carry out a difficult job, we mean that we believe that person can be trusted to carry out the job properly. It is the same with the verb, 'to believe': if I say that I believe someone, I mean that in my experience that person can be trusted to speak the truth. In all those cases we are speaking, not so much about ourselves, as about some other person.

There is no reason why it should be different when we speak about faith in God. We may have been taught to think of faith as a religious virtue, which we have, or do not have, as the case may be. But the New Testament writers knew the word 'faith' only in its ordinary meaning; and though they had been thinking deeply about faith, they were writing for people who knew only its everyday meaning. So, when they wrote about faith in God, they wanted to stress that God could be trusted.

This is true in English, but it is even clearer in Greek. For where we speak on the one hand of the 'faith' or 'trust' of the person who believes, and on the other hand of the 'trustworthiness' or 'honesty' or 'faithfulness' of the person who is believed, the Greeks had only one word for both sides of the relationship. The one word *pistis* means not only 'faith' or 'trust', but also 'reliability', 'faithfulness', 'trustworthiness', 'honesty', or an 'oath'.

And, just as in English we may say, 'the love of God', which can mean either the love which God has for us, or the love which we have for God, so Paul often wrote *Pistis Iesou*, 'the faith of Jesus', by which he could mean either 'the faithfulness of Jesus', or 'faith in Jesus'. The usual translation is 'faith in Jesus'. But Paul was not concerned with translation. To him *pistis* was not either 'faith' or 'faithfulness': the same word included both the faithfulness of Jesus and the faith of the believer. The two belong together. We can distinguish between them in our minds, but we must not separate them, and Paul certainly did not separate them. Faith, like love, is a two-way process.

So, when Paul spoke of faith, he wanted to emphasize that God, in Jesus Christ, can be trusted absolutely. He was aware that faith demands a decision on our side. We have to take God on trust. We do not see God, and we sometimes find it difficult to see His care for us in our lives and in the life of the world. There is a paradox here: we can only discover that God can be trusted, if we begin by trusting Him. Just as the proverb says, 'the proof of the pudding is in the eating', so the 'proof' of God is in trusting Him. Yet there is a good reason for trusting Him. The reason is Jesus Christ. That God, in Jesus Christ, shared our life, with its joys and sorrows, that He shared our death, even the appalling death on the cross (Phil. 2.8), that He took on Himself the responsibility for our sins (1.4; 1 Cor. 15.3), should be more than sufficient reason to trust Him. Faith is necessary for our salvation; but it is not our contribution to our salvation, for it depends entirely on God's fidelity.

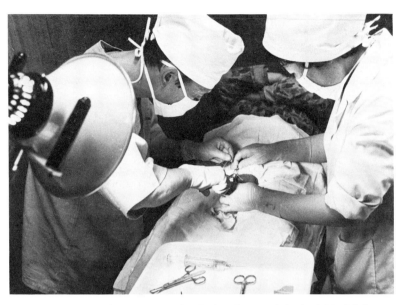

'When Paul spoke of "faith" he meant that God can be trusted absolutely' (p. 34). But we only discover that this is true if we begin by trusting Him—just as we trust our lives when we are ill to doctors and surgeons, like these in South Korea, or to the bus or train driver every time we travel, like the passengers here in Peru.

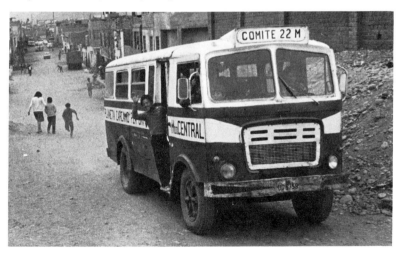

STUDY SUGGESTIONS

WORD STUDY

1. What is the chief difference between the meaning of the word 'faith' when we use it in a 'religious' sense, and its meaning when we use it in an everyday 'secular' sense?
2. In what way does the meaning of the Greek word '*pistis*', as Paul used it, differ from the meaning of the English word 'faith'?

REVIEW OF CONTENT

3. 'To say that we "have faith in someone" does not mean that we possess some quality called "faith".' What does it mean?
4. What was it that Paul wanted to emphasize, when he wrote about 'faith in God' and 'faith in Jesus'?
5. 'We do not see God ... yet there is good reason for trusting Him' (p. 34). What is that reason?

BIBLE STUDY

6. Read Mark 9.17–24. When the sick boy's father said 'I believe; help my unbelief', what do you think he meant? Was he expressing his faith or his doubt? How far does Jesus's response as described in Mark 9.25–27 help you to answer?
7. Read Matthew 17.20. What did Jesus mean by 'faith' in this passage, and how far are His words true, in your experience?

DISCUSSION AND APPLICATION

8. 'We can only discover that God can be trusted, if we begin by trusting Him' (p. 34). What are some of the ways in which we can 'trust' God in our daily lives? What are some ways in which we fail to trust Him?
9. A certain marriage counsellor tells young couples that 'marriage is just as much about faith and hope as it is about love'. Why do you think that faith and hope should be important for a successful marriage?
10. Some people ask: 'If "everything is possible to one who believes", why is it that those who believe in faith-healing are not always cured? Is it because their faith or the faith of the healer is too little? Or for some other reason?' What answer would you give them?

3.1–5

The Galatians' Earlier Experience

SUMMARY

Paul reminds the Galatians how they became Christians, and asks, do they want to exchange the Spirit for the 'flesh'.

NOTES

3.1. Bewitched. The Galatians seem to have come under a spell.
Publicly portrayed. This translation is not quite accurate, and could be misleading. The Greek verb means (1) 'to write beforehand', 'to predict' (Rom. 15.4), or (2) 'to make known through a written proclamation', 'to proclaim publicly'. Paul was asking, 'Has someone put a spell on you, in spite of the clear explanation you have had of the crucifixion of Christ?' (JB).
3.2. Hearing with faith. Paul's Greek words mean either (1) 'believing what you heard' (NIV) or (2) 'the obedience of faith', that is to say, 'acting on your faith'. It seems almost certain that Paul meant the first, but we cannot quite exclude the other (see chapters 5—6).
3.3. The flesh. The Hebrew word *basar* and the Greek word *sarx*, both meaning 'flesh', do not mean 'the body' in contrast with the soul, nor does 'flesh' mean 'the material' in contrast with 'the spiritual' (NEB), and certainly not our 'lower nature'. 'Flesh' means human beings as they actually are (see note on 1. 16). It means especially that they are not God, and that they are mortal. The contrast between Spirit and flesh is the contrast between God's work and people's own achievements. In many cases the best translation of *sarx* is 'self' (5.13, 16). The NIV translates correctly: 'After beginning with the Spirit, are you now trying to attain your goal by human effort?'
3.5. Works miracles among you. In the early Church the work of the Spirit was often accompanied by spectacular manifestations, such as speaking in tongues, 'miraculous' healings, and other 'signs and wonders'—as it still is in some Churches today. In 1 Corinthians Paul warns against attaching too much attention to such things. They are meaningful and have a place in the life of the Church, but other gifts are also the work of the Spirit, such as, for example the ability to teach, or to do welfare work without being patronizing, and above all the gift of love, which is the greatest of all (1 Cor. 12—14). Here, however, Paul makes a special point of mentioning the more spectacular gifts.

INTERPRETATION

Paul now addresses the Galatians on the contradiction between the gospel of Christ and the teaching of his opponents. He does not give their teaching in detail: the Galatians knew that already. However, we do not know exactly what it was, and we can learn only a little about it from what Paul writes. But this much is clear: they were insisting that, in order to earn God's favour, Christians had to obey certain commandments of the Jewish Law.

Paul appeals to the Galatians by reminding them of what had happened when they became Christians. They had heard the gospel proclaimed to them. His words do not claim that he had given them an impressive portrayal of the gospel events, and particularly of the crucifixion. He may have done so, but we do not know. What he says is that he presented the gospel openly and clearly and that they had accepted it.

The gospel was preached to them without any strings attached: God's grace is given freely. It was offered freely to the Jews, when Jesus worked among them, and not only to faithful Jews, but also to 'tax-gatherers and other bad characters' (Luke 15.1, NEB), that is to say, not only to those who obeyed the Law but also to the disobedient; and when Paul preached to the Galatians, he offered it without the obligations of the Law. The Galatians had received the Spirit simply by accepting God's free offer.

In contrasting the Spirit and the flesh, Paul is stressing the contrast between God's work for us, and to us, and in us, with any attempts to gain salvation by our own efforts—in the case of the Galatians by depending on certain commandments of the Law.

That the Galatians had received the Spirit was shown by the evidence of 'miracles'. There seems to have been a strong charismatic element in the Galatian Churches, including miracles of healing; indeed, Paul himself was reputed to heal the sick (see Acts 14.8–10). They could not deny that these things happened among them; and they knew that they had received these gifts because they had believed the gospel, not because they observed any Jewish laws.

These things were evidence that God had accepted them. And all this had come to them as God's free gift, which they only had to accept, and which they had accepted. Now, Paul asks, do you want to throw all this away, and start again with your own efforts? Had all that God had done for them been in vain?

STUDY SUGGESTIONS

WORD STUDY

1. 'Having begun with the Spirit, are you now ending with the flesh?' (3.3). Which of the following contrasts was Paul referring to as 'flesh' and 'Spirit' in that verse?
   (a) the body and the soul
   (b) material things and spiritual things
   (c) human achievement and God's work
   (d) our lower nature and our higher aspirations

REVIEW OF CONTENT

2. How had the gospel first been presented to the Galatians, and how had they responded to it?
3. What evidence had Paul described, which showed that the Galatians had received the Holy Spirit as 'God's free gift'?
4. What did Paul fear was now happening to the Galatian Christians?

BIBLE STUDY

5. What links can you see between Gal. 3.1–5 and Luke 15.1?
6. Paul's opponents were tempting the Galatians to depend on obedience to the Jewish Law as their means of salvation. What resemblance, if any, can you see between that temptation and the temptation of Jesus as described in Matt. 4.1–11?

DISCUSSION AND APPLICATION

7. Some Christians say that the three words 'the world, the flesh, and the devil' describe three different sorts of temptation; others say they are three ways of describing the same thing. What is your opinion, and why? Reread the note on 3.3, and then give some examples of these 'deceits' as they affect the Church and individual Christians today.
8. In 3.5 Paul referred to 'miracles' as evidence that the Holy Spirit was at work among the Galatians. What are some other signs or gifts which show that individual Christians or Church congregations have received the Spirit? What signs or gifts of this sort, if any, can you see in the congregation to which you belong?
9. How would you answer someone who asked: 'How can we believe in the truth of the gospel unless God gives us miracles to prove it?'?

God Gave the Promise before He Gave the Law

SUMMARY

Paul proves from the Scripture that justification has always been through faith in God's promise, for 'Abraham believed God, and it was reckoned to him as righteousness', and in Abraham all the nations were to be blessed.

NOTES

3.6. Abraham 'believed God, and it was reckoned to him as righteousness'. Paul is quoting from the Greek version of Genesis 15.6, which differs slightly from the Hebrew, but the meaning of both versions is the same. God had spoken to Abraham, and Abraham had believed Him, and that is what counts as righteousness in God's sight. The Genesis text does not mean that God really desires something called 'righteousness', but will accept 'faith' instead. It means that faith is all that God requires: faith *is* the righteousness which God demands, for it is the right response to His promise.

3.7. Sons of Abraham, that is to say, Abraham's people (the Jews often used 'sons of . . .' or 'children of . . .' for any sort of connection, as in expressions such as 'sons of righteousness', etc).

3.8. 'In you shall all the nations be blessed.' The quotation is from Genesis 12.3, which most modern versions translate as, 'By you all the families of the earth shall bless themselves', meaning that people will say, 'May God bless us as He blessed Abraham' (but the GNB and NIV agree with Paul's interpretation of the Genesis text). In either case, as Paul was saying, the Genesis text means that the calling of Abraham was of universal significance, as well as being of special significance to the Jewish people who regarded themselves as his descendants.

INTERPRETATION

The point of this part of Paul's argument is that he wanted to show that the right relationship between God and his people had always been governed by God's promises and the people's response in faith. When God called Abraham, there was as yet no written Law. God spoke, and Abraham believed Him (even though what God was promising him seemed unlikely), and that was all there was to it. That was 'righteousness', that was the right relationship between God and Abraham.

This did not mean that Abraham did not have to obey God. He did. God commanded Abraham, and Abraham acted upon His commands. In a sense we could say that Abraham was obeying 'God's commandments' or even 'God's Law'. But the point Paul wants to make is that God's favour to Abraham, and the relationship of faith which grew out of that favour, came first. Abraham's obedience was the outcome of his faith, not the other way round.

So, at the first stage the Law played no part at all. Paul's argument is supported by the fact that outside the books of the *torah* (the 'books of Moses') the Old Testament writers rarely refer to any specific commandments of the Laws of Moses. God's commandments were regarded as important, and people were expected to carry out God's will. When the prophets accused the people of Israel of having disobeyed God's will, they were probably thinking of specific commandments; but they rarely mentioned them as such. For example, Micah based his criticism of people's conduct on the fact that God 'has showed you, O man, what is good; and what does the Lord require of you but to do justice, and to love kindness, and to walk humbly with your God?' (Micah 6.8).

The gospel, that is to say, God's promise, came first, and for Abraham and Paul the only possible response was faith. God's promise often meets with unbelief, but the *right* response, the 'righteousness' of Genesis 15.6, is faith.

STUDY SUGGESTIONS

WORD STUDY

1. What did Paul mean by 'sons' of Abraham in v. 7?

REVIEW OF CONTENT

2. What was it that Paul wanted to show in this passage?
3. (a) What did Paul mean when he said that 'the scripture ... preached the gospel beforehand to Abraham'?
   (b) In what way was God's promise to Abraham especially relevant to Paul's argument against his opponents?
4. Genesis 15.6 'does not mean that God really desires something called "righteousness", but will accept "faith" instead' (p. 40). What does it mean?

5. Read Exod. 20.1–17 and Micah 6.8. 'When the prophets accused the Israelites of disobedience "they were probably thinking of specific commandments"' (p. 41). On which of the ten commandments do you think the prophet Micah based the 'three things' which he said that God 'requires' of us?

6. In what way does the teaching of the following passages contradict the teaching of Paul's opponents among the Galatians? Gen. 12.3; Hab. 2.4; Rom. 4.1–13.

7. Compare the words of the prophet in Micah 6.8 with those of Jesus in Mark 12.28–31. What difference, if any, do you see between the meaning of the two passages?

DISCUSSION AND APPLICATION

8. Some people ask, 'If God counts our believing in Him as "righteousness", why do we need to keep the ten commandments as well?' How would you answer them?

9. Some people claim that there is a 'natural' law which shows all people what is right and what is wrong, whether or not they believe in God or in the gospel of Jesus. How far do you think this is true? Does it mean that people of all religions have the same basic ideas about right and wrong? How far, if at all, do you think that this affects God's judgement? (See also 12.16, and Rom. 2.26–29.)

10. 'God's promise came first.' What is the significance of this statement for those who preach the gospel today?

Special Note C

Righteousness and Justification

These are two key words in Paul's thinking, so we need to look at them carefully. This is especially important because they can easily be misinterpreted, which in turn would lead us to misunderstand what Paul wrote.

1. It is tempting to regard the biblical idea of 'righteousness' as another word for 'justice', but this would be a mistake. Justice means giving everyone his or her due. A 'just' person is someone who carries out all their obligations, who treats people as they ought to be treated, who gives to all people what is owing to them, and who allows them to keep what belongs to them. A just society is a society in which all people have their fair share, and are all treated by the same rules. And a

just judge, or a just court of justice, is one which punishes the guilty, acquits the innocent, and in some cases rewards the deserving. This idea of justice comes from the Romans, whose laws were in many respects very fair, and have been an example to many nations.

But not all nations thought, or think, as the Romans did, and the Old Testament idea of 'righteousness' is different from the Roman idea of 'justice'. The Old Testament does contain similar ideas of justice. They are present, for example, in the law of the *talio* (meaning 'retaliation'): 'you shall give life for life, eye for eye, tooth for tooth, hand for hand, foot for foot, burn for burn, wound for wound, stripe for stripe'. The purpose of this law was to end the ancient custom of blood feud, and also to prevent excessive punishment. In Israel it was forbidden to kill other members of a clan simply because one member had committed a crime. It was also considered wrong to kill a man for stealing a sheep, or to cut off his hand for stealing a loaf. Punishment was not allowed to hurt the offender more than the crime had hurt the victim. But this sort of justice was not called 'righteousness', and *sedaqa*, the Hebrew word which we usually translate by 'righteousness', is never used in connection with punishment. It is actually very difficult to say exactly what *sedaqa* means. We come close to it, if we think of an atmosphere in which the right relationships can flourish.

A Hebrew word that comes nearer to 'justice' is *mishpat*, which is usually translated as 'judgement'. But in *mishpat* the emphasis is on vindicating the innocent and protecting the helpless, rather than on punishing the guilty. Note, for example, how in the case of Solomon's first judgement, nothing is said about any punishment of the guilty woman: all that was needed for a right judgement was that the child should be given to the rightful mother (1 Kings 3.16–28).

2. The Greek word *dikaiosyne*, meaning 'righteousness', also differed from 'justice'. Many Greek people did, indeed, interpret 'righteousness' as 'giving everyone their due', but this interpretation was challenged by others. The philosopher Plato, for example, argued that it could never be 'righteous' to harm people, even if they deserved it. 'Righteousness' was seeking people's true good, and above all, the true good of the community.

3. Paul was a Jew, and when he used the Greek word, he also had the Hebrew idea in mind. 'Righteousness', as he understood it, did not mean that people were good, or honest, or law-abiding, but simply that they were in the right relationship with God. He would assume that this right relationship with God would also make them good, and honest, and fair-minded, and probably law-abiding. But what made them 'righteous' was not their own goodness; it was God's goodness, His grace, which they had received through faith.

4. The words *dikaioma* and *dikaiosis*, meaning 'justification', are

'forensic' terms, that is to say, words used in a court of law. Their precise meaning is 'a favourable verdict' by a judge, or by some sort of law-court. This is usually interpreted as meaning an acquittal, or a verdict of 'not guilty'. The doctrine of justification, interpreted in these terms, means that, because of the passion and death of Christ, God acquits us of our guilt. We are all guilty before God, but, guilty though we are, God acquits us.

This interpretation stresses two important points. It takes our guilt before God seriously. When we stand before God, we are all guilty, for we have offended against His holy Law and against His holy love, and the death of Christ was needed to put us right with God. It also stresses that what really matters is God's judgement: if He declares us not guilty, then His verdict stands.

However, there are difficulties with this interpretation. We accept that what matters is God's verdict, and that He is free to judge as he chooses. But, we may ask, if we are all guilty of offending against His holy Law, how can He declare us 'not guilty'? We are taught that God's judgement is 'true and just' (Ps. 119.137; John 8.16; Rev. 19.2); but to declare the guilty 'not guilty' seems to make Him an unjust judge.

5. Part of the answer to this question is that not all court cases deal with criminal law. The words which Paul used could also be used in cases of civil law, in cases dealing with property, when the court has to decide who is the legal owner of certain property. In the ancient world this property might be a slave. Now there is strong evidence that we are slaves of sin, and the devil can show evidence that we have served him, and can claim that we belong to him (see John 8.34; Rom. 6.17; Col. 2.14; Rev. 12.10). But God the Judge decides that we belong to Jesus Christ, who 'bought' us (Mark 10.45; 1 Cor. 6.20), and set us free (4.8–11, see also John 8.36; Rom. 6.18, 22; Rev. 1.5). It would be absurd to ask, to whom Jesus paid the price. This was not a business transaction. All that the New Testament writers want to stress is that Jesus paid dearly for putting us right with God. This interpretation would bring Paul's teaching on justification in line with his teaching on redemption.

6. Some Churches use the word 'justification' in the sense of 'making people righteous'. The Greek words which Paul used cannot mean this. But we may be certain God's work of justification is effective. God does not do half work, and when Christians have been accepted by Him as His own, and in turn have accepted Him as their God, then they will repent of their wrong ways, and become new people. They still continue to stumble and fall, and in this sense they are still sinners, but they are no longer *slaves* of sin, and this will show in the new and 'godly' lives they lead.

7. In his letters Paul rarely used the words 'forgive' and 'forgiveness' (only Rom. 3.25; 4.7; and, if these letters are by him, Eph. 1.7; Col.

1.14). However, it is important to realize that his teaching implies that God has forgiven us our sins.

Parents who forgive naughty children may still demand that the children should admit their faults, and may even find it necessary to punish them; but in spite of everything, they still love their bad children as much as if they had done no wrong. Similarly God, as a loving Father, forgives our sins, and continues to love us. Whatever we may have done to spoil our relationship with Him, His attitude to us remains the same. This is the reason why He set in motion the whole work of our justification and redemption, and sent His Son into the world to live with us and die for us. It is not as if God could only forgive us because Christ died for us; it is the other way round: Christ died for us because God forgives.

STUDY SUGGESTIONS

WORD STUDY

1. 'It is tempting to regard the biblical idea of "righteousness" as another word for "justice" but this would be a mistake' (p. 42). What are some of the differences in meaning between the two words?
2. What aspect of justice is emphasized by the Hebrew word usually translated as 'judgement'?
3. What was the precise meaning of the Greek words translated as 'justification'? In which two different ways could these words be used in a law-court? Explain how these two different uses may affect our understanding of Paul's teaching about justification.

REVIEW OF CONTENT

4. What was Paul chiefly wanting to convey when he used the word 'righteousness'?
5. Why did Paul use the language of the law-courts in arguing against the teaching of his opponents?

BIBLE STUDY

6. Explain the connection between Paul's words to the Galatians in 3.11–12 and his words to the Romans in Rom. 4.13–15.

DISCUSSION AND APPLICATION

7. 'To be "righteous" is not the same as being "sinless".' How far do you think this is true? How would you answer someone who said: 'If human beings are 'all still sinners' (see p. 44) how then can anyone be 'counted as righteous'?'?
8. 'When people have been accepted by God, and have accepted Him

as their God ... they become new people' (p. 44). What are some of the ways in which this 'newness' shows—or should show—in the lives of Christians? What are some of the things which can *prevent* it from showing?

9. Some people say 'If God is ready to forgive us when we sin, there is no point in trying to be righteous.' What is your opinion?

3.10–14
The Contrast between Law and Redemption

SUMMARY

3.10. Those who rely on works of Law are under a curse.

3.11–12. The Scripture says that justification is not by Law but through faith.

3.13–14. Christ redeemed us from the curse of the Law, and brought the blessing of Abraham to the Gentiles.

NOTES

3.10. All who rely on works of the law. Paul wrote, 'all who are of works of law', but the RSV conveys the meaning of the quotation from Deuteronomy 27.26, and most translations are similar.

3.11. He who through faith is righteous shall live. Paul was quoting from memory from Habakkuk 2.4 (we do not always realize how difficult it is to look anything up in a scroll, and we do not even know if Paul had a scroll at hand to look up his quotation), and in quoting from memory one is likely to be inaccurate. The Hebrew text actually reads, 'the righteous shall live by his faithfulness' (RSV footnote, JB, NEB, REB, GNB), or '... by his faith' (AV, RSV, NIV), whilst the Greek version reads, 'the righteous shall live by my faithfulness', that is to say, by God's faithfulness. Paul may at some time or other have come across both versions, but, quoting from memory, has left out the pronoun 'his' or 'my'. Paul's quotation is translated variously as 'the righteous shall live by faith' (AV, RV, Moffatt, Phillips, JB, NIV), or, 'he who through faith is righteous shall live' (RSV, NEB, GNB). The latter translation accords well with Paul's way of thinking, but the first translation accords better with the Habakkuk text.

3.13. Christ redeemed us. This is not the Greek word which Paul

'Did you receive the Spirit by works of the law or by hearing with faith?' (3.5). Faithful believers 'will live by that relationship which depends on God's side on His faithfulness' (pp. 38, 49)—as the life of this Swiss mountain climber injured by an avalanche depends on the 'faithfulness' of the rescue team who risk their own lives to save him.

normally used for 'redeem'. It literally means, 'to buy up', but also carries the sense, 'to deliver at some cost to the deliverer'. Paul clearly did not mean that someone had to be paid or compensated for our delivery, but simply wanted to stress the high personal cost to the Redeemer.

The curse of the law. Paul does not mean condemnation by God, but the curse that is the outcome of regarding the Law as the governing principle of our relationship with God (see note on 1.8, 9 and Special Note D).

Having become a curse for us. This is a difficult phrase. Paul may have meant, (1) that Jesus had offended against the letter of the law (see e.g. Mark 2.23–28), and that He suffered for this, or (2) that Jesus experienced God's displeasure with sin, through His close friendship with sinners (see e.g. Mark 2.13–17).

On a tree. Paul actually wrote, 'on wood', that is to say, 'on a piece of timber'. The Greek word *xylon*, meaning 'wood', could be used for a tree (Rev. 22.2), but was more commonly used for dead wood, such as tree stumps, fire-wood, wooden beams or ships (or the wooden bars in a xylophone). Here the 'wood' means the Cross (as in 1 Peter 2.24).

INTERPRETATION

Paul now sets out to show that those who rely on their own achievements, and regard their obedience to the Law as the means of 'justification', place themselves outside God's promises. The danger of relying on their own goodness rather than on God's goodness, is that they create a barrier between God and themselves, and so put themselves under a curse.

Paul's next sentence adds something to this: 'for it is written, "cursed be every one who does not abide by all things written in the book of the law, and do them".' So the law cannot give any real hope, as it condemns everyone who does not do *all* that is written in it. Even if it were possible in theory to put oneself right with God through obedience to the Law, this would not work in practice, for nobody's obedience is perfect. This means that everyone is condemned by the Law.

According to Jewish belief it is possible to obey the Law. This does not mean that faithful Jews believed they were without sin; but they did believe that repentant sinners could receive forgiveness within the Law, for the Law mentioned ways to obtain forgiveness, such as the sin-offerings and guilt-offerings (see Leviticus 4—7), and the Day of the Atonement (Lev. 16). However, in this letter Paul was not fighting against Judaism, but against a deviation from the Christian faith.

In any case, the Scripture states clearly that righteousness, that is to say, the right relationship with God, comes through faith. The example of Abraham had already shown this (vv. 6–9), and it was also confirmed by the prophet Habakkuk. Habakkuk had actually written about matters which were quite different from those about which Paul was writing. Habakkuk's problem was that he had not been able to see the fulfilment of his earlier prophecies, so he wanted to examine how God worked in history. But the LORD told him, 'the righteous shall live by *my* faithfulness', or 'the righteous shall live by *his* faith' (see note on v. 11, and Special Note B). The difference between the two versions is not as great as it seems, for in either case the 'righteous', the faithful believer, will live by the relationship between God and himself which depends on God's side on His faithfulness, and on the believer's side on his faith. So Habakkuk was told not to examine how God did His work, but to trust Him.

So although Paul had something rather different in mind, he could use the same words (see Special Note B) to emphasize that God's faithfulness was shown in the death of Christ on the Cross. In Christ God came down on our side, and became one of us; He took on Himself a human life with all its pains, and also with the consequences of our sins. This act on God's part was costly and painful: as we know, it meant the Cross. The various New Testament writers emphasize, each in their own ways, how costly this was. Mark and Matthew have perhaps shown this most movingly by recording Jesus's cry, 'My God, my God, why hast thou forsaken me?' (Mark 15.34; Matt. 27.46). Even though the Psalm Jesus quoted (Ps. 22) ends in hope, the words show deep anguish. Besides the extreme physical pain, the Son of God also suffered the utter desolation of feeling forsaken by His Father. Paul did not paint such a picture here, but he too was aware of the cost, and showed this by the word he chose for 'redeemed'.

Paul does not explain here exactly *how* Jesus redeemed us from the curse of the Law, and many people are puzzled by the quotation from Deut. 21.23 in v. 13. Paul cannot have intended to suggest that Jesus, through being crucified, actually incurred God's displeasure. Nor can he have meant that Jesus was condemned to die because He had transgressed against the letter of the Law, since He was not put to death for that reason. So it seems that Paul may simply have wished to remind the Galatians of the central truth of the gospel, that in accepting crucifixion Jesus *took on Himself* the 'curse', which was the result of our disobedience to God's will. In doing this He redeemed us to enjoy the fulfilment of God's promise to Abraham in the freedom of eternal life. Many people find this difficult to understand. But we can perhaps see a shadowy reflection of what Jesus did for us in the fact that even sinful human beings are sometimes willing to lay down their lives in order to rescue or 'redeem' others from death.

So obedience to the Law is not the reason why God accepts people, and the blessing of Abraham is not confined to those who have the Law. God's favour to Abraham was a gift of His grace, and Jesus Christ through His death on the cross has extended the blessing of Abraham not only to Abraham's descendants the Jews, but also to the Gentiles, to whom He offers the same favour, and the same promise. As Abraham did, so also the Gentiles may accept God's gracious gift through their faith.

STUDY SUGGESTIONS

WORD STUDY

1. In 3.13 Paul uses a different word for 'redeem' from the word he normally uses. What is its literal meaning and what was Paul's reason for using it here?

REVIEW OF CONTENT

2. In this passage Paul points out one particular danger of relying on one's own achievements as a means of salvation. What is that danger?

3. 'Faithful Jews did not believe that they were without sin, but they did believe that forgiveness could be received within the Law' (p. 48). In what way did they believe that forgiveness could be obtained?

4. 'Our whole relationship with God depends on His faithfulness and on our faith' (p. 49). In what way or ways has God shown His faithfulness?

5. (a) What did Paul mean when he said that Christ redeemed us from the curse of the Law 'having become a curse for us' (v. 13)?
   (b) From what do we need to be redeemed?
   (c) What did Paul mean by the special word he used for 'redeemed' in v. 13?

BIBLE STUDY

6. What is the difference between the Hebrew and Greek versions of Hab. 2.4? How far, if at all, does that difference affect our understanding of what Paul was saying to the Galatians?

7. What does Matt. 27.46 tell us about the 'cost' of our redemption by Jesus on the cross?

DISCUSSION AND APPLICATION

8. Good preachers often 'preach the law', in the sense that they make it

clear what obedience to God means in the way we live our lives as Christians. How does Gal. 3.10–14 help them to avoid certain misunderstandings when they preach on this subject?

9. Some people ask 'If obeying the Law does not "justify" us, how do we know what we should do in order to be justified?' How would you answer?

3.15–22
The Law cannot make the Promise Invalid

SUMMARY

Once an agreement has been ratified, it cannot in honesty be altered or cancelled. So the promise of God to Abraham cannot be altered by the Law, which was given four hundred and thirty years later 'because of transgressions'.

NOTES

3.15. To give a human example. Paul now introduces a parable, an example from ordinary human conduct, to prove something he was saying about God's conduct, and to help the Galatians to understand his meaning more clearly.

No one annuls even a man's will. The word *diatheke*, here translated by 'will', also means an 'agreement' or 'covenant'. In the dealings between God and human beings the initiative is entirely on God's side, and this is why some translators have used 'will' (as in the RSV and the NEB). But people often alter their wills, and there is nothing wrong in their doing so. The NEB translates, 'no one else can set it aside or add a codicil', but Paul was not thinking of anyone else: he wanted to convey that God, once He had given His promise, had not made any changes to it. So it is probably better to think in terms of a covenant or an agreement: 'when two people agree on a matter and sign an agreement, no one can break it or add anything to it' (GNB).

3.16. It does not say, 'And to offsprings', referring to many; but, referring to one, 'And to your offspring,' which is Christ. Paul was referring to the accounts of God's promise to Abraham in the Jewish Scriptures (Gen. 12.7; 13.15; etc), where the collective noun meaning 'seed', 'semen', or 'offspring', is used for Abraham's descendants. This could mean one individual as well as many. Paul could not have believed that the verses in Genesis meant one person only. But knowing what God had done in Christ made him realize that the promise referred not only to the many 'seeds' who were to be blessed by it, but especially to the one 'Seed' Jesus Christ, in whom the blessing was fulfilled. But readers who look up the texts in the OT (and in Rom. 9.7 and 2 Cor. 11.22, where Paul also refers to the promise to Abraham) find that the RSV and other modern translations do not use the word 'offspring' at all, but the plural 'descendants', and so obscure the point that Paul wanted to make here. Only the NJB uses a collective noun with the same meaning, 'progeny', in both cases.

3.17. Four hundred and thirty years, according to Exodus 12.40.

A covenant. See note on v. 15.

3.19. It was added because of transgressions. This can be interpreted in various ways. (1) It could mean that the Law became necessary because of people's disobedience: it was not part of the original covenant, but was added because people did not do God's will. (2) It could mean that the Law was needed to make people realize that they were sinners: 'It was added in order to show what wrongdoing is' (GNB). (3) Some people think that Paul meant that the Law was given in order to make people transgress. (4) The NEB and REB translate, 'It was added to make wrongdoing a legal offence'. This seems the simplest interpretation, and is supported by 5.23. It would also explain why the Law forbids more things than it commands: according to the rabbis the Law of Moses commands 248 actions, and forbids 365 actions.

By angels. This is not in the Book of Exodus, but was widely believed.

Through an intermediary. The promise had been given directly to Abraham; the Law was given indirectly to Israel through Moses.

3.20. An intermediary implies more than one. This is a puzzling statement, which has been interpreted in many different ways. The simplest interpretation seems to be that one person can speak and act without an intermediary; but when two groups are involved, they usually need an intermediary. The two groups in this case are the angels who are God's messengers and the people of Israel.

3.22. The scripture consigned all things to sin. The 'Scripture' here means the Mosaic Law. Paul could mean that the Law declared that all people are sinners (see v. 10). But he probably meant that the Law could only define sins and thus show God's will more clearly; it could not *make* people either good or bad.

INTERPRETATION

This section begins with a parable. Even among humans, once an agreement has been ratified, it is binding. It may be true that unreliable people sometimes enter into agreements which they will not keep, and

'Obedience to the Law does not justify us before God' (see p. 54), but the Law can show us the sort of life He wants us to lead—rather as this Ghanaian teacher gives instruction that will guide his pupils later, when they are adult and free, or as a traffic cop in Barbados shows there are certain rules which even free people should obey for their own good and for the sake of others.

sometimes make promises which they will not carry out. But among honest people an agreement is an agreement, and must be honoured; and a promise is a promise, and must be kept. If this is true among humans, how much more will God, who is infinitely more reliable than any human, abide by the covenant which He made with Abraham, and keep the promise which He made to him.

Paul was well aware of the many times when God's covenant with Israel had to be renewed, but he was not concerned with that. His concern was to show that God could be expected to honour the promise He had made to Abraham. In Paul's view that promise pointed to Christ. The way in which he argued this may seem strange to us, but it is clear what he wanted to convey: that Jesus Christ is the fulfilment of God's promise to Abraham.

God keeps His promises. So the promise which He made to Abraham cannot be annulled by the Law, which was given so much later. If God had given a Law which would make people acceptable to Him and grant them true life, that would mean that God had withdrawn His promise. This could never be, for God is absolutely reliable; and God had never given such a Law.

But this leads to the question, 'If the Law was not meant to justify people, why was it given at all?' Paul's answer, 'It was added because of transgressions', can be interpreted in four different ways (see note on v. 19). Of those four, the last seems to be the most likely. A law, any law, 'defines transgressions'. Doing what the law forbids, or not doing what the law commands, is a transgression, which can be duly punished by suitable penalties. People do not become good by obeying the law, nor can they justify themselves before God by doing so, but obedience to the law provides a framework within which it is possible to live the kind of life which God wants us to live.

However, this framework remains empty, if it is not filled with something more than just obeying the letter of the law. The law contains numerous pointers to that 'something more', but cannot enforce it.

For example, it is important that we should not commit adultery (Exod. 20.14). But if two people are to live a good and happy married life, according to God's will, much more is needed. The love on which a good marriage is built cannot be provided by law. Similarly, we must not kill (Exod. 20.13), but it is not enough for us merely not to murder people. Such instructions as 'If your enemy is hungry, give him bread to eat, and if he is thirsty, give him water to drink' (Prov. 25.21, and see Rom. 12.20) cannot easily be fitted into any law, and cannot be enforced. And even though they are important, in showing us how love works in practice, they cannot give us the love we need (see Matt. 5.44). The list of examples could easily be extended. The verdict must stand:

the Law as given through Moses defines transgressions, but it cannot 'make alive' (v. 21): it cannot in itself *make* people love God or one another.

So the Law is good, but it is not the way by which we gain God's favour. God's favour is His free gift, not a reward for services rendered, and it does not come to us 'by legal right' (v. 18, REB). The promise God made to Abraham, and its fulfilment in Jesus Christ, were given by God in His amazing grace. The Bible writers never ceased to be amazed at God's grace. In the Church we sometimes miss this sense of wonder, though it is expressed in the well-known hymn, *Amazing Grace* (by John Newton, who, rather like Paul, had led an ungodly—and even blasphemous—life, until by God's grace he was almost literally 'made alive' by being saved, against all the odds, in a ship-wreck).

God has already accepted His people. That is all the justification they need. All that He requires of us is that we should accept His grace through faith in Jesus Christ. And that is when our obedience to the Law becomes something 'positive', growing out of our love for God and our wish to please Him, rather than out of a 'negative' fear of offending Him and suffering the consequences.

STUDY SUGGESTIONS

WORD STUDY

1. What are some other possible translations of the Greek word which the RSV translates as 'a will'? Which translation makes its meaning clearest, and why?
2. For each of the following words write a short sentence to show its meaning as used by Paul in this passage: intermediary; transgressions; covenant.

REVIEW OF CONTENT

3. In vv. 6–8, 18 (and again in v. 29) Paul emphasized that God's promise to Abraham was fulfilled in Jesus Christ. What was it that made Paul recognize and understand that this was true?
4. What is the most probable meaning of Paul's statement that God 'consigned all things to sin'?
5. (a) Why did Paul say that if Law rather than faith was meant to govern our relationship with God, this would mean that God had withdrawn His Promise?
   (b) Why did Paul reject such an idea?

6. What connection do you see between Paul's arguments in Gal. 3.15–22 and the teaching of Jesus according to Matt. 5.17–48?

DISCUSSION AND APPLICATION

7. In this passage Paul compares God's promise to Abraham with the promises people make when they enter into a covenant or agreement with each other, or give to their heirs when they make a 'will'. How far do you find that this comparison helps you to understand the connection between God's promise to Abraham in Gen. 12.2–3 and Paul's statement that in Christ we are all 'sons' of God?

8. 'If the Law was not meant to justify people, why was it given at all?' (p. 54). How far do you find that the ten commandments and any other part of the Mosaic Law helps us to live in the right relationship with God? To what extent, if at all do you find them *un*-helpful?

9. Find out more about the life of John Newton, and the incident which led him to write the hymn 'Amazing Grace'.

10. If God is faithful to His promises, what is His present relationship with the Jewish people? Find out if you can (tactfully!) what the views of Jewish people today are on this subject.

Special Note D
The Law

One of the problems in discussing the idea of the 'law', is that this word can be used in more than one sense. This was true in Greek and Hebrew just as it is in English.

1. The Greek word which the New Testament writers used for 'law' was *nomos*, which was used in a number of different ways.

(a) The word *nomos* meant every sort of custom hallowed by ancient use or tradition: the manner in which things had always been done. This included also religious custom, the way in which the gods had always been worshipped, and ought to be worshipped.

(b) The word *nomos* also meant the written law, by which justice was administered. But the Greeks did not believe that law-givers were free to invent and decree laws as they pleased (as some modern law-givers do). So the laws of the ancient Greek city-states were believed to be based on the first meaning of the word, (a), and to be of divine origin. The law was therefore the standard of conduct, and its authority was absolute. This respect for the law is illustrated beautifully by the conduct of the philosopher Socrates, when he had been condemned to death 'for preaching strange gods'. This verdict was unjust, for he was innocent, but he had been convicted according to the law, so when he had the opportunity to escape he refused to do so, for he did not wish to act against the law. It must be admitted that most people were not quite so law-abiding. Nevertheless the law was held in high respect. This meant that in the ancient Greek city-states the law was regarded as the actual 'king', no matter who the rulers were who administered the law.

(c) This changed to some extent in later times, when rulers began to be regarded as divine, so their will was 'law'.

Greek philosophers also extended the meaning of *nomos*, in two directions.

(d) First, they include the moral laws by which everyone ought to live; and because people regarded it as natural that they should do so, they called this the 'natural law'.

(e) Secondly, they discovered that in the natural world nearly everything happens in a regular manner: if you sow seeds of corn, they will produce corn, not apple trees; if you drop something, it will fall down, not up; the sun rises every morning, and sinks every evening; etc. They called this regularity of natural phenomena the 'laws of nature'.

(f) Jews and Christians chiefly used *nomos* as a translation of the Hebrew word *torah* (see below). Paul normally used it in this sense, but not always.

2. The Hebrew word *torah* means 'guidance', 'teaching', 'instruction'. It could be used for the instruction given by a teacher (Prov. 4.2), or for the guidance given by God through His prophets (Isa. 1.10); but it was used most commonly for His commandments, and for those five books which contained His commandments: Genesis, Exodus, Leviticus, Numbers and Deuteronomy.

(a) God had revealed Himself as the Ruler of His people Israel. The *torah* is an expression of His absolute sovereignty over His people, and it must be obeyed, because the LORD is Israel's heavenly King. But God is not a tyrant. He has the good of His people at heart, and His commandments are a gift of His love. Thanks to His *torah* His people knew how they could walk safely through the difficult paths of life. They could delight in His statutes, for they knew that the psalmist was right in saying: 'Thy word is a lamp to my feet, and a light to my path' (Ps. 119.16, 105).

(b) In New Testament times the Jewish attitude to the *torah* had changed. Rabbinic Judaism seems to have stressed two points: it was only in the *torah* that (1) God had revealed Himself; and (2) a person could have a relationship with Him. This could mean, and often did mean, that the *torah* was put between God and the people in such a way that He could no longer be seen as a living God. Of course, by stressing its authority, the rabbis wanted to make sure that God's will was done.

The rabbis knew, and taught, that the *torah* had not created the relationship between God and His people. That was an act of His grace. The *torah* maintained that relationship, and people could remain in fellowship with God only by observing every letter of the *torah*. But such zeal for the *torah* could mean, and sometimes did mean, that God's will was *not* done. That was the case, for example, when attempts were made to stop Jesus from healing on the sabbath, though God desired that someone should be helped at once (John 5), or when Jewish Christians threatened to split the Church at Antioch (2.11–14).

We could almost say that the Old Testament prophets had regarded Israel as the family of God, in which the Father had laid down certain rules for the conduct of His family, whilst the rabbis tended to regard people as slaves of the *torah*. This is perhaps not quite fair, as the rabbis did want to ensure that God's will was done, but they also tended to lose sight of the personal relationship between God and His people.

(c) The Gospels show that Jesus regarded the *torah* as the revealed will of God, but His relationship with the Father was not governed by it. His relationship with God was unique, but this did not mean that He was not obliged to do God's will; on the contrary, God's will meant all the more to Him because He was God's Son. And this was the crucial point: Jesus knew that the *torah* was made for people, people were not made for the *torah* (see Mark 2.27). The *torah* shows how people should behave *as a result* of being in a right relationship with God, but it could never take the place of that relationship. Jesus's obedience was the obedience of a mature son.

3. The early Christians had to deal with a new situation. It was not difficult for them to agree that the *torah* was given to Israel, and that Gentiles were not expected to live by all its commandments; that had already been agreed by the rabbis. But problems arose, as we have seen, in communities where there were both Jewish and Gentile Christians; and we have also seen how Paul thought the Church ought to deal with such problems.

But there is still the deeper question of the function of the Law, and this is where Paul made his most significant contribution, by showing the Churches that the Law must serve our relationship with Gòd, not govern it. In this he was guided both by the Old Testament and by the life and teaching of Jesus. Paul too regarded the Law as the revealed will of God, but he recognized that the relationship between God and His people had been created by God's undeserved favour. The Law had been given later to define the limits within which His family ought to live (see note on 3.19), and to show how they should behave. The Law was God-given and good. But as Jesus had shown it was not God, and in some circumstances God's will for us might override, or even be contrary to, the letter of the written Law.

STUDY SUGGESTIONS

WORD STUDY

1. Briefly describe some of the different meanings given to the Greek word '*nomos*', 'law'. How was it chiefly used by Jews and Christians?
2. (a) What is the precise meaning of the Hebrew word '*torah*'?
   (b) What are some of the ways in which it was used by writers in the Bible?

REVIEW OF CONTENT

3. (a) Why did, and do, the Jews believe that the *torah* must be obeyed?
   (b) Why did, and do, the Jews feel that they ought to be grateful for the *torah*?
4. (a) In what way did the attitude of the rabbis to the *torah* differ from that of the OT prophets?
   (b) In what way did Jesus's own relationship with God affect His actions and His teaching with regard to the *torah*?
   (c) In what ways does the teaching of Jesus with regard to the *torah* resemble or differ from that of the rabbis and that of the prophets?
5. What was the 'new situation' which the early Christians had to face with regard to the *torah*?
6. Briefly summarize Paul's understanding of the function of the Law. What did he say the Galatians' attitude to it should be?

BIBLE STUDY

7. Read Acts 15.1–29. With whose understanding of the *torah*, as described in this Special Note, did each of the following people described in Acts agree?
   (a) the 'men from Judaea'
   (b) Paul and Barnabas
   (c) Peter
   (d) the party of the Pharisees
   (e) James
   (f) the Apostles and Elders

DISCUSSION AND APPLICATION

8. What is the basis of the 'written law' in your country? How far is it based on what is assumed to be the will of God? How and by whom can it be changed? How far is the Church involved in making or administering the law in your country?
9. The Greeks believed that there is a moral or natural law, by which people know instinctively what is right and what is wrong (p. 57).

Find out, if you can, how far your own ideas of right and wrong are shared by people in your neighbourhood or area, who belong to other religions, nationalities or cultures.

10. Explain what you think our own attitude to the OT Law ought to be.

11. Some people ask: 'If Christ sets Christian believers free from Law and tradition, why should present-day Christians obey the laws and traditions of the Church?' How would you answer them? Give your reasons.

3.23—4.7

Slaves and Children

SUMMARY

3.23–29. Before Christ came, Abraham's children were under the control of the Law, but now the faithful no longer need such a 'custodian'. Moreover, in Jesus Christ not only Jews, but all believers are God's children, and heirs to God's promise.

4.1–3. As long as he is a child, the heir is in the same position as a slave, but once he has grown up, he is a free man.

4.4–7. Paul now uses the picture of the redemption of a slave. Christ came to bring about redemption and adoption, so His people are no longer slaves but children.

NOTES

3.23. Before faith came. Paul wrote, 'before *the* faith came', meaning 'the faith in Christ'; he might have written, 'before Christ came', without much difference in meaning.

3.24. Our custodian. In some households at that time it was customary to employ a slave as 'custodian' to look after the children, and to keep them in order.

Until Christ came. Paul wants to convey that with faith in Christ the believers have reached a maturity, in which they no longer need a 'custodian' to keep them in order.

3.24–26. ... Our custodian ... that we might be justified ... we are no longer under a custodian; for in Christ Jesus you are all sons of God ... you were baptised. For the Jews among the Galatian Christians the *torah* had been 'custodian', as it had for Paul. It was they whom he included with himself in the pronoun 'we' in these verses, though most of the Gentiles among them, too, had formerly been under the restraint of religious laws and customs. With the change to 'you' in v. 26, Paul was addressing *all* the Galatians, Jews and Gentiles alike. See also 'we' in 4.3–5 and 'you' in 4.6–7.

3.28. There is neither Jew nor Greek, there is neither slave nor free, there is neither male nor female. Paul did not mean that those distinctions no longer existed. There are different nations and cultures; there were slaves, and there are still people whose condition is as bad as that of slaves; and people are either men or women. But whatever our race or nationality or social status or sex, these distinctions do not affect our relationship with Christ—and as Christians ('in Christ') such distinctions should not affect our relationships with each other.

4.1. No better than a slave. In making these comparisons Paul was clearly thinking of house-slaves in a good family, rather than the gangs of slaves who worked on the estates of large landowners, or those who worked in the mines under appalling conditions, or as galley-slaves. House slaves were regarded as part of the family, but they did differ from the children. Under Roman Law all prisoners of war, before being sold into slavery, underwent a ceremony in which they were deprived of their personality, so henceforth they were regarded, not as people, but as things. They could legally be ill-treated, sold, or killed. Though they were part of the family, they could be discarded, if they were no longer wanted, so their position was never secure. Jewish Law, however, regarded slaves as human beings, and directed, among other things, that slaves must not be thrown out if they wanted to stay with the family they had served (Exod. 21.5–6).

The heir. Usually, when a man died, his son or an adopted son would inherit his possessions (Abraham, we may recall, declared that if he had no son his heir would be one of his slaves, Eliezer, who was obviously regarded as very much one of the family, see Gen. 15.2–3 and note on 4.5 below).

4.2. Until the date set by the father. When the father thought that the time was ripe for the boy to take his rightful place, the custodian would no longer be needed.

4.3. The elemental spirits of the universe. This is a term derived from Greek philosophy, which can also be translated as 'elemental principles' (NIV, NJB) or 'ruling spirits' (GNB). In any case, Paul was referring to the powers or 'gods' of the Galatians' former religion, and particularly to the sun, moon and planets, which were regarded as mighty 'gods', both among the Greeks and in local cults of that region (see note on 4.8).

4.4. Born of woman, born under the law. Paul stresses that Jesus was born under exactly the same conditions as other human beings.

4.5. To redeem means 'to purchase', 'to buy'; the word could be used

for any purchase, but was used especially (1) for ransoming a prisoner
of war, and (2) for buying a slave with the purpose of setting him free.
Adoption as sons. The 'redemption' of a slave was often followed by
adoption. Sometimes the owner of a slave would free him and adopt
him, thus making him a member of the family. Or someone else might
buy him and adopt him as a son of a new family. Adoption was taken
very seriously; the children of household slaves were often adopted as
children of the family, and it was believed that an adopted person
actually *became* the son or daughter of the adopting parents.

4.7. If a son, then an heir. This is not clearly defined. Paul simply
meant that, being God's children, we receive all that He had promised
to Abraham.

INTERPRETATION

At first sight this passage appears confusing, for Paul is using two
different pictures, which he seems to be mixing up. He first speaks of
children, who are in a position similar to that of slaves, until they grow
up; and then he speaks of the redemption of a slave. But he had good
reasons for using the two different pictures, and in fact he did not mix
them up.

The Jews were very proud of being children of Abraham (see John
8.33, 39), and heirs to God's promises, and therefore God's children.
Paul admits this: they are children of God's family, and heirs to God's
promises. But he argues that they were nevertheless in the same
position as slaves, for they were kept under control by the Law (see
2.4), which acted as their custodian. This does not mean that the Law
was a means of oppression, on the contrary, the Law is holy and good
(see Rom. 7.12). Children need to be disciplined; so God's children
needed the Law. But the training of children is not an aim in itself: the
aim of all training and education is to produce free and responsible
adults. So it is with the Law; it was not an end in itself, but was given
with the purpose of producing free and responsible adult believers.
Christ is the end of the Law (see Rom. 10.4), not as if He made the Law
invalid, but because He brought about the emancipation of His people.
He came, not to abolish the Law and the prophets, but to fulfil them
(Matt. 5.17; see also Rom. 3.31). The freedom which Christ gives was
the aim of the Law.

The Gentiles on the other hand, before they heard the gospel
message, 'were slaves to the elemental spirits'. Their religion meant that
they too were in bondage, to powers or principles of the material
universe which were not God (see 4.8). The practice of religion, any
religion, usually means observing certain rules. The Latin word *religio*,

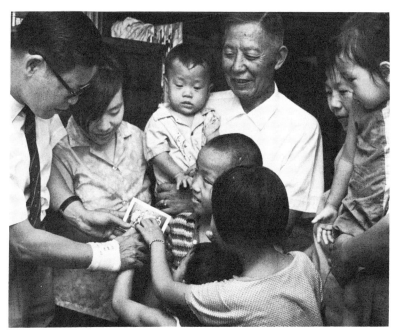

'If you are Christ's, then you are Abraham's offspring, heirs according to promise . . .
You are sons . . . crying "Abba! Father!"' (3.29; 4.6). Paul was trying to show that God's
children all belong to one family, governed by mutual love, like the members of this
family in Hong Kong, lovingly showing a family photograph to a family friend. What is
the greatest gift we receive as sons and daughters of God 'according to promise'?

'religion', means a 'bind', and the word expresses very well, that religion binds people by limiting their freedom. That was the position of the Galatians before they heard the gospel: they were kept in subjection by their religion. But Christ has redeemed them, set them free, and made them God's children by adoption.

So, Paul argues, whatever may be the differences between Jews and Gentiles, the coming of Christ has had the same effect on both. He has emancipated both Jews and Gentiles, and in relation to Christ, 'there is neither Jew nor Greek, neither slave nor free, neither male nor female.' How seriously he took this, is shown by the fact that he wrote, '*we* were slaves to the elemental spirits of the universe'. Unlike the Gentile Galatians, he had never served 'elemental spirits', but he had been subject to the material constraints of the Mosaic Law, so that any difference between himself and the Galatians was irrelevant. God had sent His Son to redeem both 'those who were under the Law', and those who had served other gods.

The statement that 'you are all one in Christ Jesus', was of great importance, for at that time the distinctions between people were taken very seriously. We have already noted the segregation between Jews and Gentiles, advocated by the Jewish visitors to Antioch. The Greeks divided the human race into Greeks and 'barbarians', and on another occasion Paul insisted that the gospel concerned both Greeks and 'barbarians' equally (Rom. 1.14). According to Luke, Paul taught that God 'made from one every nation' (Acts 17.26).

The difference between free people and slaves was regarded by many as fundamental. The Greek philosopher Aristotle had argued that a slave was merely an animate piece of property, and *by nature* different from a free person; and we have already seen (note on 4.1) that Roman Law provided for a ceremony by which slaves were deprived of their personality. Jewish Law, indeed, regarded slaves as people, but in Paul's days even a Jew might have been surprised at Paul's advice to Philemon: 'Receive (Onesimus) back for good—no longer as a slave, but as more than a slave: as a dear brother' (Philemon 16, REB).

The difference between men and women is, of course, a natural one. But here too Paul maintains that they are equal in their relationship with Christ. It is unavoidable that this verse should be quoted frequently today in discussion between those Churches in which men and women can serve equally in the ordained ministry, and those which have an exclusively male ministry. Some people ask whether Paul himself realized the implications of his words. From 1 Cor. 14.34–36 it seems that he did not, but there are some problems with these verses. They interrupt Paul's argument, and may refer to something about which we know nothing (perhaps some specific women, maybe 'prophetesses' who preached strange teachings?). On the other hand, we do know the names of some women whom Paul counted among his collaborators: Lydia (Acts 16.14–15), Prisca (Priscilla, Acts 18.2; Rom. 16.3; 1 Cor. 16.19), Phoebe (Rom. 16.1), perhaps also Mary, Julia, Tryphaena, Tryphosa (Rom. 16.6, 12, 15), (and possibly Junia, Rom. 16.7, AV, REB, though RSV and other translations have the form Junias). But we do not know in what functions they collaborated with him.

Important though the issues are, which are raised by 3.28, we must not lose sight of the purpose for which Paul wrote this verse. He was trying to show that God's children, men and women, free and slave, Jews and Gentiles of every nation, are *one* family, governed by mutual love. In v. 5 he had mentioned some 'charismatic' gifts as evidence of the Spirit, here he digs deeper: the great gift of the Spirit is the love by which we enter into that intimate relationship with God, which makes us cry, 'Abba, Father'.

STUDY SUGGESTIONS

WORD STUDY

1. What is the precise meaning of the word 'redeemed' (4.5), and for what was it especially used?
2. What do you understand by the word 'slavery'?
3. What does the word 'custodian' mean, as used in 3.24–25?

REVIEW OF CONTENT

4. What was the position of slaves in a good household in NT times, and what was the essential difference between a slave and a child?
5. What did Paul mean by the statement that 'the law was our custodian . . . but now that faith has come we are no longer under a custodian' (3.24–25)?
6. In what way did Paul mean that our redemption by Jesus resembles the custom of adopting slaves as children of the family?
7. What did Paul mean by 'elemental spirits of the universe' in 4.3, and in what way were both Jews and Gentiles 'slaves'?

BIBLE STUDY

8. In what way does the teaching of Paul in Gal. 3.23—4.7 reflect the teaching of Jesus in John 8.31–38?
9. Which of the following passages contains the same teaching as Gal. 3.27–28?
   John 17.20–23   Rom. 2.17–21   Rom. 12.4–5   Acts 17.26–27
   1 Cor. 10.16–17   Phil. 1.27   Phil. 2.9–11

10. When Paul talked about slavery in 3.28, do you think he was talking about slavery as a condition of life, or only in a religious or spiritual sense? Why do you think it was not until many centuries later that slavery as a condition of life was abolished in countries calling themselves Christian? How far do you think that Churches and individual Christians should be concerned to abolish social evils?

11. Many people today use Paul's statement that 'in Christ ... there is neither male nor female' to support their belief that women as well as men should be ordained as ministers or priests. How far do you think this was what Paul—or his hearers—had in mind? What is the practice of your own Church in this matter? What is your opinion on the subject, and why?

12. What was the chief difference between Jews and Gentiles in Paul's time? What, if anything, can (a) Churches and (b) individual Christians do today to break down barriers between people of different nationalities, cultures and races, either within the Church or in the community as a whole?

13. Mature adults, though they are free and responsible, if they are wise, will practise what they learned as children. Explain what this means as regards the Law and the Christian life.

4.8–20

Paul's Concern for the Galatians

SUMMARY

4.8–11. Before the Galatians knew Christ, they were slaves of powers which are not God. Paul cannot understand why they now want to return to that condition of slavery, and wonders if his work amongst them had been in vain.

4.12–16. He reminds them of their regard for him when he preached the gospel to them, and asks if they now regard him as an enemy because he has told them the truth.

4.17–20. He appeals to them not to be deceived by the flattery of his opponents, and stresses his concern for them.

NOTES

4.8. Beings that by nature are no gods. Paul does not deny the existence

66

of the 'gods' of the Gentiles, but asserts that they are not the one true God. Religions were not 'invented' because people wanted to indulge their imagination. In most religions people try to keep on good terms with realities over which they have no power. In many religions people worship the sun because of its power to give warmth and light, to make things grow, but also to cause droughts and famines. Mother earth feeds her children with grains and fruit. Clouds give refreshing and life-giving rain, but also bring frightening thunderstorms and terrible floods. Other forces are more subtle but equally strong, such as for example the sexual urge, which exercises tremendous power over people. All these powers or material 'principles' seem to be capricious, they can work for good or for evil, and people feel it is important to keep them friendly, or, if they are hostile, to pacify them and to make them friendly. As many of these powers or 'gods' are connected with the year of nature, the calendar plays a large part in many religions, which makes the observance of the stars and planets an important matter: the proper seasons must be observed, and the proper ceremonies must be performed, otherwise, so people believe, terrible things might happen. When some natural disaster strikes, such as an earthquake, or a dry summer leading to a poor harvest and famine, or a plague of locusts, or an epidemic among people or cattle, people always wonder what they have done wrong: has some ceremony been forgotten, or performed wrongly? Religious observances are often festive and cheerful, but an element of fear plays an important part.

4.9. To be known by God. Paul was writing in Greek, but he was a Hebrew (2 Cor. 11.22; Phil. 3.5). In Hebrew 'to know' also means 'to love'. It is often used for 'making love', or 'having sexual intercourse', but can be used for many different sorts of love; the emphasis is on the closeness and intimacy of the love.

4.10. Days and months, and seasons, and years. This seems to show that Paul's opponents laid great stress on the observance of the Jewish calendar. Judaism differs from many religions in that its annual festivals, which were originally connected with the seasons of sowing and harvest, have become days to remember and relive *historic* events, that is to say, God's saving acts in history. God's salvation had freed Israel from the idea that religious observance can influence nature. These festivals are observed at the proper time, and in the proper form, but they celebrate the freedom which God gives. However, in Paul's days there were some Jewish sects in which the seasons had again become the masters, and astrology played a large part, with ideas about the good or bad influence of time and chance, and of the planets, on human affairs.

4.12. You did me no wrong. This translation seems to suggest that the Galatians had treated Paul well when he preached the gospel to them, but were doing him wrong now. But Paul may have meant, 'You have done me no wrong' (NIV), meaning that he did not feel that he had been personally insulted by their conduct even now.

4.13. Because of a bodily ailment. Paul's words mean literally 'through weakness of the flesh', but we have no way of knowing what his ailment or disability was. We only know that it must have been something unpleasant to see, so that people might have wanted to shun him. The 'thorn given me in the flesh' (2 Cor. 12.7) may have been the same thing.

4.14. You did not scorn or despise me. Paul actually expressed himself more strongly: 'You did not spit on me'.

An angel of God. The Greek word *angelos* means a 'messenger'. It is used for a human messenger in Luke 7.24; 9.52; James 2.25, but in the New Testament it usually means a heavenly messenger (e.g. in Luke 1.11; Romans 8.38; Rev. 1.1; etc).

4.15. You would have plucked out your eyes. Some interpreters think that this hints at the nature of Paul's ailment; but it is picture-language, meaning that they would have done anything for him.

4.19. Little children. Paul used only one word, a diminutive, meaning 'little children'; but this translation is perhaps too literal. Paul did not mean that the Galatians were only little children in the faith, but used this word as a term of endearment, to show that they were dear to him. Earlier in his letter he had stressed that they were no longer little children (3.23—4.7).

INTERPRETATION

The Galatians had once been 'in bondage' to powers and principles which were not God. But they had heard the gospel, and had come to know God, or rather, they had learned that God knew them, that is to say, loved them. Since they had become God's children, enjoying the freedom of His children, Paul could not understand how they could possibly wish to return to a condition of slavery. By observing 'days, and months, and seasons, and years' the Galatians were reverting to ways which were very similar to their former practices. They had, in fact, not become more Jewish, but less so. Paul had no objection to setting certain days apart for worship and prayer (Rom. 14.5–6), but he was strongly opposed to people doing this in order to pacify God—as if God needed to be pacified.

Paul now appeals to the Galatians to become as he is, and accept the same freedom by which he lives, for he has become as they are. He had shown this freedom in the way in which he lived as a Jew, when he was among Jews; but to the Gentiles, who were outside the Law, he became as a Gentile (1 Cor. 9.19–23), in other words, he adapted himself to the people among whom he worked. For many people this is one of the most difficult things they have to do, and perhaps especially for those in the Christian ministry. When people arrive in a new environment, they often find customs which are different from those they have been used to, even including differences in the way people live their Christian lives. This means they have to decide which of their old customs they may rightly abandon, and which new customs they should adopt, always examining their own consciences, but also remembering that they do not have to earn God's favour by religious observances. This was a problem early Christians had to face all the time. They had to adapt themselves to the customs of the people among whom they worked, without becoming unfaithful to their Master, Jesus.

Paul saw that ministers of the gospel must stand alongside their people. You can only proclaim the forgiveness of sins if you are yourself a sinner who has been forgiven, and if your people know this; you can only truly comfort people in their grief, if you feel the same pain which they feel; you can only guide people properly, if you stand where they stand, so that you can walk together. And you cannot really stand beside people, if you show, or pretend, all the time that you are different.

This is one side of the matter. The other side is that the people so guided must walk with their guide. He is by their side, but if they refuse to walk with him, they will either stay where they are and get no further, or they will go astray. So Paul urges the Galatians to walk with him.

In the next few verses Paul reminds the Galatians of his ministry among them. He remembers that time with gratitude, and he has no quarrel with them. But he is wondering whether their affection for him has changed because he has told them the truth.

Paul warns the Galatians against being deceived by the flattery of his opponents, who had probably told the Galatians that they could become 'superior' Christians by following their rules. He also points out that 'strict' preachers often seek their own glory. People derive a lot of satisfaction from telling other people what to do, and are often honoured for it. We can see this clearly in the way in which the leaders of some 'strict' sects enjoy the power which they have over their followers, and in the honour in which their followers hold them. Some years ago there was the example of Jim Jones, who founded a new sect and organized them in a community in Guyana. When he told his followers that they had no place in the present world, and that they ought to kill themselves and their children, this was exactly what most of them did: they committed suicide and killed their children. That was an extreme case, but it illustrates the power and hold which religious leaders can have over their followers.

But Paul was not really interested in his opponents. He was interested in his 'little children' (v. 14) and anxious to see them develop as true Christians. He wished he could be with them again, and able to soften the harsh tone of his letter by showing his love for them. As things were, he simply did not know what best to say to them.

STUDY SUGGESTIONS

WORD STUDY

1. What is the full meaning of the word 'know' as used by Paul in 4.8–9 to describe the relationship between God and the Galatians?

REVIEW OF CONTENT

2. In what way were the Galatians reverting to their former religions?
3. What did Paul mean by 'beings which are by nature no gods'?
4. (a) For what chief reasons have 'days and months and seasons and years' been regarded as important in many religions?
   (b) For what other reason do some religions, and especially Judaism, relate their worship and festivals to 'times and seasons'?
5. In what ways did Paul say he had adapted himself to the people among whom he worked?
6. What had been the relationship between Paul and the Galatians when he first visited them, and in what way had it changed?
7. What did Paul suspect were the real motives of his opponents in their dealings with the Galatians?

BIBLE STUDY

8. Which verse from this passage did Paul express more fully in 1 Cor. 9.19–23?

DISCUSSION AND APPLICATION

9. 'Brethren ... become as I am, for I have become as you are'. In what situations today is it especially important for Christian ministers and missionaries to 'become as' those to whom they minister? What are some of the steps they need to take in order to do so?
10. The 'Christian Year', with its seasons of Advent, Christmas, Lent, Easter, Ascension and Pentecost (and usually a Harvest Festival) evolved in northern countries. What relation do these 'seasons' of religious observance bear to the seasons of nature? What difficul-

ties, if any, does this cause for Churches with different seasons and climates?

11. Paul in 4.19 addressed the Galatians as 'My little children', and in some Churches it is customary for Church members to address the clergy as 'Father'. In what circumstances do you think it is acceptable for a Christian leader to regard fellow Church members as 'children'? What are some of the titles which different denominations use to address their leaders, and what do these titles show to be the relationship of those leaders with their congregations?

4.21—5.1

Children of the Slave and Children of the Free Woman

SUMMARY

4.21. Those who wish to be under the Law ought to listen to the Law.
4.22–23. Abraham had two sons, one by a slave, and one by a free woman. The son by the free woman was the child of the promise.
4.24–31. 'The present Jerusalem' is like the slave woman, but 'our mother', the 'Jerusalem that is above', is free.
5.1. Christ has set His followers free 'for freedom', so the Galatians must not submit again to a yoke of slavery.

NOTES

4.21. You who desire to be under law, do you not hear the law? Paul was using the word 'law' in two different meanings. The first time he meant the commandments of the Law, the second time the 'books of the Law', which we call the 'books of Moses'.

4.22. One by a slave and one by a free woman. The story of Abraham's two sons is told in Genesis 16, 17 and 21.

4.23. According to the flesh, that is to say, in the ordinary way.

Through promise. Sarah had already passed the age at which women ordinarily cease to conceive children, but God had promised that she would bear a son, and He keeps His promises. Paul takes this to mean that all God's promises would be inherited by Sarah's son and his heirs.

4.24. This is an allegory. The word 'allegory' is used for a story or picture-language in which each character or image stands for some idea or quality. Paul did not mean that Sarah and Hagar had not been real people; he was using the story of the two women to emphasize a deeper spiritual truth.

Mount Sinai, where Moses received the Law (Exod. 19).

4.25. In Arabia. The precise location of Mount Sinai is not known, and was almost certainly not known to Paul. He probably simply thought of it as somewhere away to the south.

The present Jerusalem ... is in slavery with her children. This is a difficult expression. The usual interpretation is that Paul was referring to Judaism, but in his view the Jews were not slaves, though they were equally restricted by the Law, like children still under a 'custodian' (3.24; 4.1–2). Other interpreters think Paul may have meant the Church in Jerusalem, but he had already made clear that he had no quarrel with that Church (2.1–10).

4.26. Jerusalem above, that is to say, the heavenly city of God, of which the Christians are citizens (Phil. 3.20).

She is our mother. Paul seems to have thought of the Christians as citizens of the heavenly city, temporarily living on earth, like the Jewish communities in Gentile cities, and Greek settlements in 'barbarian' cities. Today we might make the comparison with groups of Arabs living in African cities, Caribbeans in British cities, and Chinese in cities all over the world. 'Jerusalem above' was the 'mother city', and the Churches were 'settlements' on earth.

4.28. Isaac was Abraham's son by Sarah.

4.29. Persecuted him. This is a rather strong interpretation of Genesis 21.9, which merely states that Ishmael was teasing Isaac (but the RSV translation of the Genesis verse, 'playing with her son Isaac', is too weak).

INTERPRETATION

There is reason to suspect that parts of this passage are not exactly what Paul wrote, but it is difficult to work out exactly what may have been altered or added, perhaps by a copyist who found it a difficult passage, and tried to make it clearer.

But the purpose of the passage is clear: Paul wanted to illustrate the contrast between slaves of the Law and God's free people by another example from the Old Testament. He was firmly convinced that 'Jerusalem above is free, and she is our mother', and that Christians are citizens of heaven (see Phil. 3.20). They live on earth, but they carry the passport of the heavenly city. Jerusalem above is the Mother City of the Christian Church. The same idea is expressed somewhat differently in Revelation 20.9; 21.2, 10, and may have been familiar among early Christians. The writer to the Hebrews describes the Old Testament faithful as pilgrims on the way to their heavenly homeland, which suggests a similar idea (Heb. 11.13–16).

Allowing that some of the details of this passage are perhaps not exactly as Paul wrote them, it seems clear that in his view the example of Ishmael and Isaac showed that God's promise created free children. This freedom had been given to the Galatians, yet they were stupid enough (3.1, REB, NJB) to want to be slaves.

STUDY SUGGESTIONS

WORD STUDY

1. What is an 'allegory'? What is the difference between an allegory and a parable?

REVIEW OF CONTENT

2. What did Paul mean when he spoke in this context of 'slaves', and exhorted the Galatians not to 'submit again to the yoke of slavery'?
2. 'Paul had no quarrel with the Jerusalem Church' (p. 72). How do we know this?
4. Paul used the story of Abraham's wife Sarah, and his slave-girl Hagar, and their sons Isaac and Ishmael 'as an allegory'. In that allegory, what did Ishmael and Isaac respectively stand for?
5. What did Paul mean when he said that 'the Jerusalem above is our mother'?

BIBLE STUDY

6. In what way can Phil. 3.20 and Rev. 20.9 add to our understanding of this passage?

DISCUSSION AND APPLICATION

7. What are some of the ways in which the 'rules' by which we live our Christian lives, and the 'rules' laid down for us by the Church, may endanger our freedom 'in Christ' and make 'slaves' of us? What can we do to avoid this danger?
8. Christians 'live on earth, but they carry the passport of the heavenly city' (p. 72). How would you explain this statement to someone wishing for information about the Christian Church?
9. Is your Church congregation or area linked to a 'mother Church'? If so, what is the relationship with the mother Church and what are the practical advantages or disadvantages, in your opinion?
10. How far do you think it is helpful to think of the Church as a whole as our 'spiritual mother'? Give your reasons.

Christian Freedom

SUMMARY

5.1. Since Christ has set us free, so that we should be truly free, the Galatians must not accept again a yoke of slavery.

5.2–4. If the Galatians allow themselves to be circumcised, they separate themselves from Christ.

5.5–6. Righteousness comes through the Spirit, in faith working through love.

5.7–12. The Galatians were doing well, so Paul hopes that they will come to their senses. He asserts that he does not preach circumcision, and suggests that those who do preach circumcision should go the whole way, and castrate themselves.

5.13–15. Christian freedom is freedom to love.

NOTES

5.2. If you receive circumcision. Paul means, 'if you allow yourselves to be circumcised' (JB, GNB).

5.3. He is bound to keep the whole law. This had evidently not been made clear by Paul's opponents.

5.6. Love. The Greek language, which is very rich, has different words for various sorts of love: *eros* for passionate love, and especially for the love between a man and a woman; *storge* for love within the family, e.g. between parents and children or brothers and sisters; and *philia* for the love between friends, and generally between people who like each other.

Jews and Christians, however, preferred to use another word, *agape*, which was rarely used by other people. The Greek translators of the Old Testament probably started this. We do not know whether they chose this word deliberately, but it did have certain advantages. Most sorts of love are either spontaneous, or grow naturally. They are also selective, and therefore limited in scope. Men usually feel passionate about some women (or preferably one woman) but not others, and women feel passionate about some men (preferably one man) but not others. The members of a family do not *choose* to love each other, they just do love them, and though they may sometimes quarrel violently, this does not mean that they cease to love one another. We have to admit that there arc families whose members do not love each other, but this is unusual. And we cannot help liking some people, and not liking others.

The Christian love, *agape*, on the other hand, embraces *all* those who come our way. *Agape* includes love for people whom we do not like, and even for our 'enemies' (Matt. 5.44). Of course it is better to 'love one another with brotherly affection' (Rom. 12.10); but even if we cannot *like* some people, we can still *love* them with *agape*. *Agape* can be tender and affectionate, and even passionate (the word occurs frequently in the Greek version of the Song of Solomon); but even when it is not, we can still seek the true good of both friends and enemies, of the people we like, and those we do not like.

5.7. You were running well. The Greek word was used especially for what we should now call track events in the stadium. The Galatians had a good chance 'to win the prize'.

5.9. A little leaven leavens the whole lump. As Jesus Himself pointed out (Mark 8.15), even a small amount of leaven, or yeast, will spread through a large amount of dough. In the same way, for the Galatians to accept the one rule of circumcision as necessary for their justification, will make them once again subject to the whole of the Law, and poison and destroy their whole relationship with Christ.

5.11. But if I, brethren, still preach circumcision. Paul's opponents may have said that Paul himself believed that circumcision was necessary, and sometimes preached accordingly, but had not told the Galatians.

5.12. Mutilate. The Greek word means, to 'cut off', and was used specifically for castration.

5.13. Not ... the flesh, but ... love. The manner in which Paul's opponents misused the Mosaic Law created a divisive concern for the ego, the self, the 'flesh'. Paul contrasts this with the true freedom created by Christ's law of love.

INTERPRETATION

Paul now begins to explain what Christian freedom is like, stressing that it is the gift of God, so that nothing we do, or allow others to do to us, can add anything to it. However, for Gentiles to allow themselves to be circumcised, as his opponents had evidently urged the Galatians to do, was not only unnecessary, but would be the wrong thing altogether. In itself circumcision is neither an advantage nor a disadvantage for our salvation (v. 6), but if we try to use it as a means to gain salvation we show that we think that Christ is not enough, and so separate ourselves from Him (v. 2). Paul was not saying that a circumcised person cannot be saved; he had himself been circumcised (Phil. 3.5, and see note on 2.3). But circumcision can add nothing to what we have received in Christ.

Paul sees circumcision, and with it the whole law and all attempts to justify ourselves, as denying the sufficiency of God's grace. He did not deny that faith should be active. Faith is God working in us, and the Christian life must be *lived* (v. 6). By the gift of God's grace and through faith, we have been set free to do His will, and this freedom is the basis of Christian living. Paul's great objection to the teaching of his opponents was that their insistence on the letter of the Law, as a means of justification, actually offended against the Law and threatened the Christian love which is God's will.

God's will is that we should love our neighbour as ourselves (v. 14). But we cannot do this if we direct all our efforts towards making ourselves good, trying to earn God's favour and gain a front seat for ourselves in heaven. If we do good to other people in order to become better people ourselves or to earn God's favour, then we are not really loving them, for we are doing it for our own benefit and satisfaction, not for their good. Love means that we have other people's interest at heart, rather than our own.

This love is made possible by God's grace. Once we believe and know that Christ has redeemed us, and that we do not need to worry about adding anything to that, then we are free to love, and can begin to care for others.

God's grace is not confined to the Church; we often find *agape* among people of other religions or no religion, who have been touched by God's goodness without knowing it. But those who *have* learned about God's grace, and yet try to justify themselves, put true love out of their reach.

Jesus and the Pharisees agreed, and Jews and Christians still agree, that love for God and our neighbour is the chief commandment of the Law (Lev. 19.18; Deut. 6.5; Luke 10.27). Paul followed his Master in this, but in this passage he stresses the love for our neighbour, and does not even mention the love for God. Perhaps his opponents talked much about loving God, but did not see that loving God cannot be separated from loving people. In any case Paul's chief concern was to put an end to the strife and lack of love which were making the Galatian Christians 'devour one another'.

'Religious' people are often inclined to separate the love of God from the love of people. 'Pa' van der Steur, the founder of a children's home in Indonesia, was once asked whether he devoted his life to the care of neglected or abandoned children for the love of Jesus, or for the love of those children. He had to answer that he did not know—and this was as it should be, for we must not separate the love of God from the love of

'Through love be servants of one another' (5.13). This love is made possible through God's grace—and God's grace is not confined to the Church: these Indian women giving money and food to beggars are Hindus. But if our almsgiving and other 'acts of charity' are done simply to gain merit or earn God's favour for ourselves they actually separate us from His love. What *more* does Christ demand of those He has 'set free to love'?

human beings; whatever we do for anyone who needs us, we do for Jesus (Matt. 25.31–40).

God does indeed reward deeds of love (though not by 'giving us rewards'). But if the chief motive for what we do is the hope of reward, there can be no love. A religion of law is a work of the 'flesh', for it is concerned with self. In spite of their stress on the letter of the Law, Paul's opponents were offending against its chief commandment, which is the commandment of love.

STUDY SUGGESTIONS

WORD STUDY

1. In what chief way does the meaning of the word '*agape*' differ from that of other Greek words for 'love'? How does this make it especially useful for describing Christian love for one's neighbour?

REVIEW OF CONTENT

2. God's will is that we should 'love our neighbour as ourselves'. What is meant by the statement that this sort of love is 'made possible by God's grace'?
3. In what way does attempting to justify ourselves before God conflict with our relationship of love for Him and for other people?
4. If 'neither circumcision nor uncircumcision is of any avail' (v. 6), why was it wrong for the Galatians to allow themselves to be circumcised?
5. In what way does the attempt to gain salvation by obeying the letter of the Law actually offend against the Law?

BIBLE STUDY

6. (a) What is the chief difference between the teaching of Jesus according to Mark 12.28–31 and Matt. 22.34–40 and Paul's teaching in Gal. 5.14?
(b) In what way might the teaching of Jesus in Matt. 25.31–40 help to explain that difference?

DISCUSSION AND APPLICATION

7. What different sorts of love are distinguished in the language of your country or culture, and what words are used to describe them? Is there a word similar in meaning to the meaning of '*agape*' as used by writers in the NT? If not, how do people describe that sort of love in your language?
8. Three hundred years ago, translators of 1 Cor. 13 used the word 'charity' for '*agape*' in the 'King James' or Authorised Version of

the Bible. What does the word 'charity' usually mean in modern English, and how far does it relate to the idea of Christian love for one's neighbour?

9. 'God's grace is not confined to the Church; we often find *agape* among people of other religions or no religion' (p. 76). Give some examples of *agape* that you have yourself experienced from people of other religions. What reason do you think they would have given, if asked, for loving others in that way?

10. One student said, 'If God's grace is not confined to the Church, why should we become Christians?' Another said, 'The best reason for loving other people is that God loves them too.' What is your opinion?

11. Christians are sometimes accused of running schools and hospitals and development schemes, not because they love people but because they want to persuade them to become Christians. How would you answer such criticism? How does it compare with what Paul was saying about his opponents in Gal. 4.16–18?

5.16–26
The Works of the Flesh and the Fruit of the Spirit

SUMMARY

Paul contrasts the works of the flesh with the fruit of the Spirit.

NOTES

5.16. The flesh. 'Flesh' does not mean our 'lower nature' (NEB— which has been revised to 'unspiritual nature' in REB). Just 'human nature' (GNB) comes closer to what Paul meant, and 'Self' is probably the best translation (see note on 3.3).

5.17. To prevent you from doing what you would. This is a difficult phrase. Paul may mean that the opposing influences of the Spirit and the 'flesh' create a conflict within every Christian: our self-will tries to stop us from obeying the Spirit, but the Spirit counteracts our self-will. However, this interpretation is not certain.

5.19. The works of the flesh are plain. This introduces a catalogue of vices such as we often find in ancient writings. These lists were traditional, so we need not think that Paul's opponents indulged in all of them. However, he may have included some because of what his opponents taught or did, and 'strife' and 'dissension' clearly describe what was happening among the Galatians (v. 15).

Fornication. The Greek word meant sexual intercourse with a prostitute, but was used generally for all sexual intercourse between people who were not married. The early Church regarded the life-long relationship between one man and one woman as supremely important (see Mark 10.11–12; Matt. 5.31–32). Paul regarded any offence against this relationship as very serious, because it offended, not only against a rule, but against love.

Impurity. The Greek word could mean anything that was dirty. Paul meant careless sexual relationships.

Licentiousness. The Greek word means 'unruly conduct'.

5.20. Idolatry, i.e. the worship of images; but Jews used it for the worship of other gods than the God of Israel.

Sorcery, i.e. the use of witchcraft, spells or potions.

Enmity is hostility between people, and

Strife is the quarrelling which results from such enmity.

Jealousy. The Greek word *zelos* could mean 'jealousy', but it usually means 'zeal', especially 'excessive zeal'. This must be what Paul meant, as jealousy is covered by the word 'envy' in v. 21.

Anger. The Greek word can mean any sort of feeling or emotion, but strong feelings often lead to anger, and this must be what Paul meant.

Selfishness. This translation is questionable. The Greek word was used for in-fighting about positions of honour. 'Selfish ambition(s)' (NEB, REB, NIV) is better.

Dissension and **party-spirit** were two faults against which the Galatians had to be warned.

5.21. Drunkenness and **carousing** were rare in ancient Israel, and the Gospels contain only one warning against them (Luke 21.34). The Greek word translated 'carousing' meant a festival in honour of the god Bacchus, but was also used for wild drinking parties.

The kingdom of God. This phrase, so common in the Gospels, was rarely used by Paul. When he did use it, he usually connected it with the conduct of the Christian life. In this he followed the practice of the rabbis, who stressed that God is King now, and connected the Kingdom of God with obedience to God. In this text Paul may have wanted to stress that citizens of the Jerusalem above (4.26), where God is King, ought to live and act as citizens of His Kingdom.

5.22. Love, joy. Love comes first, as being the 'incentive' (see Phil. 2.1–2) for the other qualities which characterize life in the Spirit, with joy (the Greek word denotes *great* joy) second only to the love which inspires it.

Peace is not merely the absence of strife. Though Paul was writing in

Greek, he would also have thought of the Hebrew word *shalom* (see note on 1.3).

Patience. The Greek word has a variety of meanings: patience to wait a long time, long-suffering to tolerate other people's faults, endurance to bear suffering, and perseverance to carry out a difficult task.

Kindness. The Greek word suggests 'usefulness', but was generally used for 'kindness', with the idea that kindness is practical and helpful.

Goodness is a very general term, and really includes all the others in this sentence.

Faithfulness. The Greek word *pistis* includes both sides of a relationship of trust; so it means both 'faith' and 'faithfulness'. See Special Note B.

5.23. Gentleness. Paul's conduct makes it clear that he did not mean softness. The Gospels show that Jesus too, gentle though He was, was not soft (Matt. 12.34; 23.13, etc).

Self-control, see Proverbs 16.32.

Against such there is no law. This seems to confirm our interpretation of 3.19, above.

INTERPRETATION

It may seem at first as if Paul is here contradicting himself. Throughout this letter he has been arguing that Christians are set free from bondage to the Law, and now he is himself laying down the law, telling people what to do, and what not to do. But Paul never suggested that freedom from the Law meant that we need not obey God. On the contrary, by redeeming God's people Christ has set them free to obey God's call to love, and there is no law against love. So the Law is no longer needed to keep us in bondage, though it does still serve as a guide.

Without Christ people are 'in the flesh', and separated from God, they tend to be chiefly interested in themselves. The fourth-century theologian Augustine of Hippo once aptly defined sin as 'the heart turned in on itself'.

This does not always show itself in vices. Some very religious people are interested only in their own salvation and nothing else, so that although they behave in a religious way and obey all the rules of the Church, they are still in the flesh. The law, however, can deal only with those 'works of the flesh' which are actually vices, and try to prevent people from committing them.

It is absurd for people whom Christ has redeemed still to go on doing the works of the flesh, but Paul knew very well that even though Christians are led by the Spirit, they are still tempted by works of the flesh. Just as the Israelites in the wilderness sometimes yearned for the 'fleshpots' of Egypt, forgetting that in Egypt they had been slaves (Exod. 16.3), so Christians are tempted by sin, forgetting that sin means slavery (see John 8.34). And we fall for temptation again and again. So Paul urges the Galatians not to succumb to the works of the flesh, but to accept and enjoy the fruit of the Spirit.

The list of vices is not meant to be complete. Like similar lists it contains only selected examples. Most of them seem to have been chosen at random, but the middle ones are connected with the troubles in Galatia. By giving specific examples, Paul has avoided the trap, into which many preachers fall, of being so vague, that no one applies the words to themselves. They are like Calvin Coolidge who when asked what a minister had said in a sermon on sin could only reply: 'He said he was against it.' Paul too was 'against sin', but he tried to make sure that his readers should recognize their own sins.

Enmity, strife, excessive zeal, selfish ambition, anger, and party spirit threatened the life of the Churches in Galatia. There is nothing wrong with zeal for a good cause, but our zeal must be positive, and we must not treat people who disagree with us as enemies to be vanquished. Organizing ourselves in groups or parties is often necessary, and may be the best means of achieving necessary social, political or religious change. But it becomes harmful if we put the interests of our own party or group before all else. In Revelation 2.2–7 the Church at Ephesus is praised for its 'zeal' for the truth, but also criticized for its lack of love. And dissension between rival Christian groups can seriously damage the 'health' of the Church today, especially in countries where Christians are a small minority among strong traditional or other religions.

In one of the earliest Christian writings outside the New Testament, a letter written towards the end of the first century to the Church at Corinth, Clement, a bishop of Rome, warns the Corinthians against a 'revival of that wicked and ungodly *zelos*, by which, indeed, death came into the world' (1 Clement 3.8). He uses the word *zelos* in a wide sense, covering excessive zeal, rivalry and envy (see note on 5.20), and points to examples in the Old Testament of noble people suffering through the zeal or the envy of others. Clement continues: '... let us take the sublime examples of our own generation. Through excessive zeal and envy the greatest and most righteous "pillars" were persecuted, and battled to the death. Let us set before our eyes the good apostles. Owing to wicked zeal Peter suffered, not once or twice but many times, and thus bore witness and went to the glorious place which was his due. Owing to zeal and strife Paul gained the prize of endurance.' (1 Clement 5.1–5). He then refers to other victims of persecution, and ends this section of his letter with the general observation, 'Excessive zeal and strife have destroyed great cities and uprooted mighty nations' (1 Clement 6.4).

'Excessive zeal, selfish ambition, party spirit' (5.20 and see p. 82) are all works of the flesh which we condemn when we see politicians promising justice and peace—as here in Calcutta—and then, in some cases, when they gain power oppressing and exploiting people. And it was these same 'desires of the flesh' in Paul's opponents that were threatening the Church in Galatia. How can we prevent them from leading to strife among Christians today?

The passage is unclear, because it refers to things which Clement obviously expected the Corinthians to know about, but which we do not know. However, it seems clear that at a time of persecution, probably under Nero in AD 64, some 'Christians' were prepared to betray to the authorities fellow-Christians of whom they disapproved. The later history of the Church also shows many sad examples of excessive zeal leading to strife among Christians, often causing the deaths of innocent people.

Paul contrasts the works of the flesh with the 'fruit of the Spirit'. He speaks of 'fruit' in the singular, because what the Spirit gives is not a number of different things, but a new life, characterized by certain qualities and full of joy, in which the chief aim is 'to glorify God, and fully to enjoy Him for ever'.

However, life in the Spirit is not an easy option. It is given to us, so it is not the *result* of hard work, but it calls for much hard work, and often suffering too. Love often meets with hostility. As Christians in a largely secular or non-Christian world we may suffer scorn from unbelievers, or persecution by the state. And proclaiming the gospel requires a lot of patience, for we may not see the results until the next life. Those who live by the Spirit follow a crucified Lord.

Paul knew also that the fruit of the Spirit does not come automatically. The new life must be accepted and practised: so, 'if we live by the Spirit, let us also walk by the Spirit' (v. 25).

STUDY SUGGESTIONS

WORD STUDY

1. In 5.19–23 Paul lists the 'works of the flesh' and the 'fruit of the Spirit'.
   (a) What is the chief difference in meaning between 'works' and 'fruit', and why did Paul use 'works' for the flesh and 'fruit' for the Spirit?
   (b) Why did he use 'works' in the plural and 'fruit' in the singular?
2. What is the usual meaning of the Greek word '*zelos*', and what is its full meaning as used by Paul in this letter?
3. Which *four* of the following words or phrases are nearest in meaning to St Augustine's description of sin as 'the heart turned in on itself'?

   self-centredness   inwardness   inner life   egotism   inversion
   selfish ambition   self-respect   introversion

REVIEW OF CONTENT

4. (a) In what way may it seem as if Paul is contradicting himself in the passage?
   (b) How would you explain that Paul is *not* in fact contradicting himself here?
5. What did Paul do to ensure that the Galatians would apply his words about 'works of the flesh' to themselves?
6. For what reason did Paul put love and joy first among the features of life in the Spirit?

BIBLE STUDY

7. In which verse or verses of this passage does Paul's teaching reflect the teaching of Jesus according to (a) Matt. 11.29–30 and (b) Mark 10.21?

DISCUSSION AND APPLICATION

8. Why do we so often find the 'works of the flesh' rather than the 'fruit of the Spirit' in congregations to which we belong, in relationships between Churches—and in our individual lives?
9. Clement of Rome described how 'excessive zeal can lead to strife among Christians' (p. 82). In what way, if any, do Churches in your country, or individual Christians of your acquaintance, show excessive zeal? How can we distinguish between concern or 'zeal' for truth, and lack of love?
10. What sort of behaviour would you find in (a) a congregation characterized by works of the flesh, and (b) a congregation characterized by the fruit of the Spirit?
11. Which one of the 'vices' listed by Paul in this passage do you think is the greatest danger to the Church today, and why is it so?

6.1–10

The Law of Christ

SUMMARY

6.1–5. Bear one another's burdens.
6.6. Share with those who teach.
6.7–8. Whatever anyone sows, that he will also reap.
6.9–10. Do not grow tired of doing good; but do good to all, especially to your fellow Christians.

NOTES

6.1. If a man is overtaken, that is to say, if anyone is caught in the act, or discovered committing some crime.

Spiritual, that is to say, led by the Spirit. This is true of every Christian: Paul was not thinking of some special sort of person.

Restore him. The Greek word simply means 'repair' (in Matt. 4.21 it is used for mending fishing nets), but it was also used for restoring relationships, making peace between people.

6.6. All good things. That is, shelter, food and other necessities of life. Compare the words of Jesus in sending out the Twelve to heal and preach (Matt. 10.9–11; Luke 10.5–8).

6.7. God is not mocked, that is to say, He cannot be cheated (JB) or deceived. The Greek verb means, 'to mock', 'to treat with contempt', but the words which follow show what Paul meant.

Whatever a man sows, that he will also reap. If you sow rice, you will not harvest corn.

6.10. The household of faith. That is, the Church.

INTERPRETATION

This passage follows naturally from what Paul had said before. People who are 'under the Law' are forever finding fault with each other. This makes it possible for them to look down on others, and to be proud that they are not like other people. If they are religious, they may even thank God that they are not like other people (see Luke 18.11). Such people think that they are something, and do not realize that they are nothing.

The 'Law' of Christ is different. He wants people to bear each other's burdens. This holds good generally: He wants us to stand by people in their difficulties; but Paul was thinking particularly of the burden of people's sins. Christ did not segregate Himself from the sinners, and even objected to being called 'good' (Luke 18.19); He was a friend of sinners (Matt. 11.19; Luke 15.1).

It may seem strange that Paul here speaks of 'the law of Christ', after having said so clearly that Christ has freed His people from the Law. But free people are not lawless. They merely follow a different sort of law: they are not bound to a rigorous set of rules, but obey the will of a living Lord.

So it is not our business to criticize others, but rather to help them bear the burden of their problems, their sins, and their shame. But it *is* our business to criticize our own actions. This is what Paul meant when he wrote 'every one must bear his own load': that everyone is responsible for his own actions.

Paul now moves to another point. Within the Church certain people have specific tasks, such as teaching and preaching. This may take up a lot of time and energy, and leave them little time to earn their living. Other members, who do earn money, must be ready to share their resources with those who cannot. The early Church had no paid clergy or ministry. Paul himself always tried to earn his living by working at his trade of tentmaking (1 Cor. 4.12), but he makes it clear that those who devote their lives to the ministry of the gospel ought to have their needs provided for.

Paul ends this passage by urging the Galatians not to get tired of 'well-doing'. Even if we serve people for love, and are not working for any reward other than that of knowing that we are doing God's will, we can sometimes become disheartened, and it may encourage us to know that 'in due season we shall reap', that is to say that our work of love will bear fruit.

'Doing good to all people, and especially to those who are of the household of faith' may sound like a sort of collective selfishness: look after your own people first. But to be fair, it would have been very wrong for the small and poor early Church, to go in for wide-ranging welfare work, while expecting people outside the Church to care for starving members of its own congregations. It would have been equally wrong for members individually to undertake all sorts of 'good works', but to take no notice of the needs of fellow Christians. Their communion at the Lord's Table also meant a community in which, when one suffered, all suffered (1 Cor. 12.26).

It is very noticeable that the tone of Paul's writing has changed in the course of this letter. After the fiery beginning, and another outburst of anger in the middle (3.1–3), he ends by being quite tender. He really did care for his 'little children'.

STUDY SUGGESTIONS

WORD STUDY

1. In what way does Paul's use of the word 'law' in 6.2 differ from his use of it in other parts of this letter?
2. What was the 'load' which Paul said each person must bear for themselves?

REVIEW OF CONTENT

3. What was Paul's particular concern in 6.1–5, and how does it relate to his teaching in 3.23—4.7?

4 (a) In v. 2 Paul said: 'Bear one another's burdens.' In v. 5 he said: 'Each man will have to carry his own load.' Does this mean he was contradicting himself? If not, how should we reconcile the two statements?

(b) In what ways can we 'Bear one another's burdens', and in what circumstances do we have to 'bear our own load'?

5. What did Paul mean by 'he who sows to the Spirit'? What will such a person 'reap'?

BIBLE STUDY

6. Which verses in this passage reflect the teaching of Jesus in:
(a) Matt. 7.1–5? (b) Luke 18.9–14?

DISCUSSION AND APPLICATION

7. What are some of the ways in which vv. 1–5 apply to the practice of the Christian life?

8. What did Paul mean when he said that each one's reason to boast should be 'in himself alone'? In what circumstances, if any, do you think that Christians should 'boast' of their achievements? In what circumstances, if any, may 'silent modesty' be 'false modesty'?

9. What are some of the temptations to which 'religious' people are particularly subject?

10. What does v. 10 mean (a) for the life of the Church itself, and (b) for the work of the Church in the world?

11. According to an English saying, 'Charity begins at home'. What do you think this means? How, if at all, do you think it relates to Paul's words in vv. 9–10?

12. What are the advantages and disadvantages of Christian ministers being paid by (a) the central authorities of the Churches or denominations to which they belong? (b) the individual congregations which they serve? or (c) earning their own living?

13. In what ways, if any, do the ministers or other members of your Church 'restore' those who trespass? In what ways do they 'bear one another's burdens'? What more, if anything, could they do?

6.11–18
Ending

SUMMARY

6.11. Paul remarks that he is writing in his own hand.
6.12–15. He repeats some of his earlier warnings.
6.16–18. Greetings.

NOTES

6.11. With my own hand. Paul usually employed secretaries to write his letters. The Letter to the Romans was written by Tertius (Rom. 16.22), 1 Corinthians 1.1 contains greetings from Sosthenes, and 2 Corinthians and Philippians from Timothy, so it seems reasonable to think that Sosthenes and Timothy acted as Paul's secretaries. Similarly it seems that either Silvanus or Timothy wrote the Letters to the Thessalonians for him. No second writer is mentioned in the Letter to the Galatians, so Paul may have written this letter entirely by his own hand, but it also seems possible that he wrote only the final greetings himself.

6.13. Do not themselves keep the law. Paul may have meant that even the most religious person is not free from sin; this would be true, but it is more likely that he meant that his opponents stressed *only some* of the commandments of the Law.

6.14. The world has been crucified to me and I to the world. Paul here emphasizes that the only thing which Christians can boast of is the cross of Christ, which sets us free to 'crucify the flesh' (5.24) and live by the Spirit (see notes on 5.16–17).

6.16. The Israel of God. This means the whole people of God. Paul was not thinking of a 'new Israel' as distinguished from the 'old Israel', but of God's people Israel being extended to include all the nations (see Rom. 11.17–18; Rev. 7.1–14).

6.17. The marks of Jesus. The Greek word *stigma* means (a) a 'stab' or a 'sting'; (b) a 'brand' (to indicate who owned an animal); or (c) a 'tattoo'. As Paul would have shared the Jewish objection to tattooing (Lev. 19.28), this meaning seems excluded. It is just possible that Paul shared with some Christian mystics, including St Francis of Assisi, the rare phenomenon of having in his hands the *stigmata* of Jesus, the marks of the nails of the Cross. But most scholars believe that Paul was here referring to the wounds which he had suffered during his ministry. However, it was sometimes said that people who belonged to the God of Israel carried His 'mark', the 'mark' in this case being picture-language (Exod. 13.16; Isa. 44.5; Ezek. 9.4), so it is possible that Paul may have been referring to his baptism, which 'marked' him as belonging to Christ (though the Septuagint does not use the word *stigma* in any of the verses mentioned).

6.18. Brethren. See note on 1.11.

INTERPRETATION

Paul ends his letter by repeating and stressing some of the points he has made earlier, and adds what he suspects to be the motives of his opponents. One motive is the desire that 'they may glory in your flesh': they want to be able to boast that they have managed to convert the Galatians properly, by making them carry the outward sign of belonging to Israel: i.e. circumcision.

Another possible motive was the hope that, by remaining outwardly as Jewish as possible, 'they may not be persecuted for the cross of Christ'. At the time when Paul wrote, Christians were regarded as belonging to a Jewish sect. The Jewish faith was a *religio licita*, a legally permitted religion; indeed, Julius Caesar, the first Roman emperor (died 44 BC) had granted the Jews special privileges. As long as Christians were regarded as converts to Judaism, they enjoyed the same privileges. Paul may have guessed that the Christians might lose those privileges as soon as the authorities learned to distinguish between Jews and Christians. Clearly, if all Christians were circumcised, it would be much more difficult for outsiders to see the difference between them and the Jews.

But Paul had already made it clear, not only that circumcision was pointless for a Gentile, but also that insistence on circumcision was a denial that the Cross of Christ was sufficient for salvation. So if Paul's gospel carried the risk of persecution, it would be persecution for the Cross of Christ. In fact, this is precisely what began to happen a few years later. Paul himself is believed to have been a victim of the first large-scale persecution (in Rome in AD 64).

The fact that Paul's opponents observed only parts of the Law may be linked to the way in which the Law is a burden to a Gentile. To a Jew living in a Jewish environment, the Law ought not to be a burden, but a 'light to his path' (Ps. 119), and one of the Jewish festivals is aptly called *simhat torah*, the 'joy of the Law'. But in a different environment the Law does become a burden, and when that happens, people try to get away with as little obedience as possible. Even the most legalistic Christians do not insist on every commandment of the Law.

Over against the boasts of his opponents, Paul cannot put up any claims for himself. He is not his own man, for he belongs to his Master Christ. But although we do not know what is precisely meant by 'the marks of Jesus', it is surely relevant that a *stigma* also means a brand of ownership.

The letter ends without any personal greetings to or from individuals. Some interpreters regard this as a sign of coldness. But, true to his rather mercurial temperament, after its reproachful, even angry, beginning, Paul's tone became much warmer and gentler in the course of this letter. His reason for not adding any personal greetings may have been that he did not want to single out any one person for special attention: the Galatian Christians were *all* his brothers and sisters. And surely he could not have sent any more cordial greeting than 'the grace of our Lord Jesus Christ'.

STUDY SUGGESTIONS

WORD STUDY

1. What did Paul mean by 'the Israel of God'?
2. (a) What are three possible meanings of the Greek word '*stigma*' which is translated as a 'mark' in v. 17?
   (b) What are the possible meanings of Paul's statement that he bore on his body 'the marks of Jesus'?

REVIEW OF CONTENT

3. 'I am writing to you with my own hand' (v. 11). Why was it important that Paul should write part of the letter himself, rather than leave it all to a secretary?
4. What may have been the motives of Paul's opponents in trying to persuade the Galatians to 'rely on works of the law'?
5. In what way might circumcision have shielded the early Christians from persecution?
6. Explain the meaning of Paul's statement in v. 14 that 'the world has been crucified to me, and I to the world'.

BIBLE STUDY

7. In Gal. 6.4 Paul said 'let each one test his own work', and here in 6.16 he wishes 'Peace' for 'all who walk by this rule'. What connection, if any, do you see between the 'work' and the 'rule' Paul was talking about in Gal. 6 and the 'works' described in Jas. 1.22–25 and 2.26?

DISCUSSION AND APPLICATION

8. What is likely to happen when people regard the Law as a 'burden'? Give examples from your own experience.
9. Some Churches and Christian groups measure their 'success' by the number of other Christians whom they have 'converted' to their own way of thinking and worship practices. What was Paul's opinion of Christians who do this? What is your own opinion?
10. Some people suggest that baptism has become for Christians what circumcision is for the Jews. How far do you think that this is true? In what way does the Church's teaching on baptism relate to Paul's statement in 6.16 that 'neither circumcision counts for anything, nor uncircumcision, but a new creation'?
11. (a) How far, if at all, do Christians in your country today think of the Church, or themselves within it, as 'the Israel of God'?
    (b) How far do the members of your own Church regard themselves and the members of other Churches as 'all one in Christ Jesus' (3.28)?

Postscript

Having come to the end of Paul's Letter, we have seen that he wrote it with a definite purpose: to counteract the effect on the Galatians of certain people's preaching. We do not know in detail what they preached, but we can learn from this letter that they insisted that we can only be justified before God, if we first fulfil certain conditions. In their case these conditions included circumcision, and some other commandments of the Jewish Law. Paul regarded this as a danger to people's relationship with God, and with each other; and in order to show, and to guard against, this danger, he had to get right to the heart of the gospel.

The gospel is the message of God's good will, His love, His favour towards us (Luke 2.14; Rom. 5.8; 1 John 4.10; etc). Many religions teach that the powers, or the gods, are not necessarily favourable to us, and that it is necessary to make them favourable, that the favour of the powers or the gods must be bought, and the price may be high. The Canaanites, for example, would sacrifice their children in times of emergency, to buy the favour of their gods. But the God of Israel, the God and Father of our Lord Jesus Christ, cannot be bought. There is nothing that we do not owe to Him already. As a medieval banker, Cosimo de Medici, 1389–1464, expressed it, 'Never shall I be able to give God enough to put Him down in my books as a debtor'. The good news is that we need not try to buy God's favour, for He loves us, and is already on our side (Rom. 8.31). So He offers us His favour freely, for nothing. Any attempts to buy Him, whether by 'works of Law', or by any other means, can only spoil our relationship with Him.

The obstacles to our relationship with God lie on our side, not on God's side. These obstacles are serious, so serious that they needed the Cross to overcome them. Paul did not say much about this in his letter, but simply reminded the Galatians that he had already spoken clearly to them about it (see note on 3.1). Christ died for us, because God loves us.

As Paul sees it, the only proper response to God's grace is for us simply to accept the gift of His love, in faith, for if we do not accept the gift, we cannot enjoy it. So justification is by grace, through faith. We do need faith to enjoy God's gift, but we cannot boast of our faith, as if it was good of us to accept God's gift.

Faith implies repentance, and Paul certainly regarded repentance as an important aspect of faith (Rom. 2.4; 2 Cor. 7.9; 12.21). The very fact that he was preaching the gospel shows that he himself had repented of

92

'God has set us free from fear ... and from the letter of the Law' (p. 94)—rather like these Afghan prisoners, released from jail in a government amnesty and looking forward to regaining their political freedom. But in Christ we are also released from sin, and 'called to freedom ... to walk by the Spirit'.

his former life (1.13; 1 Cor. 15.9); but he evidently did not find it necessary to say much about it in this letter.

However, he did find it necessary to show the purpose of Christian freedom. In Christ God has set us free from fear, from the power of sin, and from the letter of the Law. That is the negative side. The positive side is that we have been set free to love and to serve God and our fellow human beings.

Christian freedom means an active life. Also, it follows certain rules, above all the law of love. Free from a blind slavery to precise regulations, and from a grim determination to be good at all costs, love will lead us to seek the true good of all those with whom we are in contact.

The Letter to the Galatians, together with that to the Romans, has often been used as a 'source-book' of Christian doctrine. This is legitimate up to a point, but only up to a point, for Paul's purpose was practical. Though our situation today differs in many ways from that of the Galatian Christians, these practical matters still concern us.

The demand that Christians should be circumcised connected God's favour with one particular nation and one particular culture. It is true that God had chosen Israel to play a significant part in His plans, but it is also true that the election of Israel was meant to serve the whole human race (Gen. 12.3; Mic. 4.1–3; etc). Later Christians have not always been as careful as Paul was in making it clear that God in Christ accepts people as they are. Many people think, quite wrongly, that the Christian faith is tied up with a particular culture. This is a great mistake, and sometimes leads to quite absurd practices. It has happened that missionaries to tropical countries offered their prospective converts trousers for the men, before they ever mentioned the gospel. We may laugh at their naive belief that trousers are more 'godly' than loincloths, but behind it lies the idea that faith is bound up with culture, which it is not (Rom. 3.29). Most readers can probably think of other examples, perhaps less ridiculous, but equally harmful.

The conflict at Antioch (2.11–14) points also to the danger of segregating Christians into groups. This would have resulted in there being two sorts of Christians, those who followed the Law of Moses and those who did not, and the first group would inevitably have regarded themselves as the better Christians. Such a division into 'first class' and 'second class' Christians can appear in various forms. In Corinth, and in some Churches today, there were 'charismatics', people who had received some specially spectacular gift of the Spirit, such as speaking in tongues. Paul valued these gifts very highly, but warned the people who had received them not to regard themselves as a special class of Christians because they spoke in tongues, while others did not. Today Christians differ among themselves in many ways, and some

Christians, or groups of Christians, do have gifts which others seem to lack. But the gifts of the Spirit are given for the whole of God's people, to serve the whole body (1 Cor. 12—14). And the Church is one body.

Some people wonder at Paul's omission of the first part of the commandment of love (5.14; see Deut. 6.5 and Mark 12.29–31). Paul knew that the love of God comes first. But so did the Galatians, so there was no need for Paul to remind them of this. Moreover, the Galatians were anxious to show their love for God by insisting on circumcision, the sabbath, and other 'religious' commandments of the Law. Further emphasis on 'love' of God might only have increased this misplaced ardour. Paul was concerned to show that a proper love of God becomes active in people's love for one another. God is not interested in religion but in people.

Paul may also help us to find an answer to the question: Why do so many Christians *not* bear the fruit of the Spirit? His answer may be that many people have not accepted God's love, for if they did, this love would transform them. It would give them great happiness, and the desire to make others happy. Paul knew that the Christian life was not easy. His own life was hard. But it was also a life full of joy, as well as a life of service freely and gladly given.

Key to Study Suggestions

Introduction

1. See p. 1, paras 2 & 3. **2.** See p. 1, para. 3.
3. (a) See p. 1, para. 2; (b) See p. 2, lines 1 & 2.
4. See p. 2, para. 2.

1.1–5

1. See p. 4, note on 1.1. **2.** See p. 5, note on 'and peace'.
3. See pp. 4–5, note on 'the Churches in Galatia'.
4. See p. 7, paras 1–3. **5.** See p. 4, notes on these phrases.
6. See p. 7, para. 3; p. 8, para. 2.
7. See p. 7, paras 4 & 5; p. 8, para. 1.
8. (a), (c) & (g) refer to (ii); (b), (e) & (f) refer to (i); (d) refers to (i) or (ii).

1.6–10

1. Distort, deform, misteach.
2. See p. 10, note on 1.8, 9. **3.** See p. 11, para. 3.
4. See p. 12, para. 1. **5.** See p. 11, note on 1.10.
6. See p. 10, note on 1.6; p. 11, para. 2.
7. See p. 11, paras 3–5.

1.11–24

1. See p. 14, note on 1.11.
2. See p. 14, note on 1.16. **3.** See p. 15, para. 2.
4. See p. 15, Interp., para. 2, especially lines 3–9.
5. See p. 15, paras 4–6.
6. See p. 14, note on 1.12, and notice especially Acts 9.3–5, 13–16.
9. See p. 15, paras 2 & 3.

Special Note A: Grace

1. See p. 17, paras 2–5; p. 19, paras 1–3.
2. Mercy, favour, loving-kindness, condescension, forgiveness.
3. (a) & (b) See p. 19, para. 5, and also p. 15, para. 3, lines 3–5.

2.1–10

1. See p. 22, note on 2.3.
2. See p. 22, note on 'that they might bring us ...'.
3. See pp. 21–22, note on 'lest somehow ...'.

4. (a) See p. 23, numbered paras 1–3, and paras. 5 & 6.
(b) See p. 23, last 2 paras; p. 25, para. 1.
5. See p. 22, note on 'was not compelled . . .'.
6. See p. 23, numbered para. 1.
7. See p. 23, numbered paras 1–3; p. 25, paras 3 & 4.
8. All 4 passages are about richer Churches helping poorer ones.

2.11–21
1. See p. 28, note on 'by works . . . through faith'.
2. See p. 29, para. 2.
3. (a) & (b) See p. 29, para. 5; (c) See p. 30, para. 2.
4. See p. 30, para. 2. **5.** See p. 29, para. 4; p. 30, paras 2 & 3.
6. See p. 31, para. 3.
7. See p. 28, last 5 lines, p. 31, paras 2 & 3.
8. See p. 28, note on 'then I prove . . .'; p. 31, para. 5.
9. See p. 30, para. 4. **10.** See p. 27, note on 2.14.
11. Peter seems to have been rather impulsive, and inclined to act without thinking.

Special Note B: 'Faith' according to Paul
1. See p. 33, para. 3. **2.** See p. 34, para. 3.
3. See p. 33, para. 3.
4. See p. 34, paras 3–5, esp. para. 5. **5.** See p. 34, para. 5.
6. This man clearly did not put much trust in his own 'faith', but he did trust Jesus to help him. Jesus showed that He can be trusted.

3.1–5
1. See p. 37, note on 3.3. **2.** See p. 38, paras 2 & 3.
3. See p. 38, paras 3, 5, 6. **4.** See p. 38, para. 6.
5. The gospel was offered without any conditions.

3.6–9
1. See p. 40, note on 3.7.
2. See p. 40, last 2 lines; p. 41, para. 1.
3. (a) See p. 41, para. 1; (b) Paul's opponents insisted that the Law was necessary for salvation.
4. See p. 40, note on 3.6.
6. All 3 passages teach that righteousness, and God's blessing, do not depend on the Law.

Special Note C: Righteousness and Justification
1. See p. 42, numbered para. 1; p. 43, paras 1 & 2, and numbered para. 2.
2. See p. 43, para. 3. **3.** See p. 44, para. 1 & numbered para. 5.

4. See p. 43, numbered para. 3. **5.** See p. 44, paras 2 & 3.
7. See p. 40, note on 3.6.

3.10–14
1. See p. 46, 48, note on 3.13; p. 49, para. 2.
2. See p. 48, para. 2. **3.** See p. 48, para. 4.
4. See p. 49, paras 1 & 2.
5. (a) & (b) See p. 49, para. 3; (c) See pp. 46, 48, note on 3.13; p. 49, para. 2.
6. See p. 46, note on 3.11; p. 49, para. 1.
7. See p. 49, para. 2.

3.15–22
1. See p. 51, note on 'no one annuls . . .'.
3. See pp. 51–52, note on 3.16.
4. See p. 52, note on 3.22.
5. See p. 54, para. 3.
6. See p. 54, paras 3–5; p. 55; and also 5.16—6.10.

Special Note D: The Law
1. See p. 56, paras 1–6.
2. (a) See p. 57, numbered para. 2; (b) See p. 57, sub-para. (a).
3. See p. 57, sub-para. (a).
4. (a) See p. 57, sub-para. (b); p. 48, first 2 paras.
   (b) See p. 58, sub-para. (c).
5. See p. 58, numbered para. 3. **6.** See p. 58, last para.
7. (a) The rabbis—but more extreme than the rabbis; (b) and (c) Jesus; (d) the rabbis; (e) tried to mediate between the two views; (f) James.
11. Take into account p. 25, para. 5 and p. 29, para. 3.

3.23—4.7
1. See pp. 61–62, note on 4.5. **2.** See p. 61, note on 4.1.
3. See p. 60, note on 3. 24. **4.** See p. 61, note on 4.1.
5. See p. 62, para. 3. **6.** See p. 62, para. 4; p.64, paras 1, 2.
7. See p. 61, note on 4.3.
8. Both passages teach that Jesus sets people free, and makes their position in the family secure.
9. All except Rom. 2.17–21 and Phil. 1.27.

4.8–20
1. See p. 67, note on 4.9; p. 68, para. 2.
2. See p. 67, note on 4.10; p. 68, para. 2.
3. See pp. 66–67, note on 4.8. **4.** See pp. 66–67, note on 4.8.

5. See p. 69, para. 1; also 1 Cor. 9.19–23.
6. See pp. 67–68, note on 4.12; p. 69, para. 4.
7. See p. 69, para. 5.   **8.** 12a.

4.21—5.1

1. For allegory see p. 71, note on 4.24; for parable see p. 51, note on 3.15, and p. 52 last 3 lines and p. 53 lines 1–6.
2. See p. 62, para. 3; p. 72, para. 3.
3. See p. 23, numbered paras 1–3.
4. Isaac represented those who relied on God's promises; Ishmael represented those who relied on 'works of law'.
5. See p. 72, notes on 4.26, and para. 3.

5.1–15

1. See p. 74–75, note on 5.6.   **2.** See p. 76, paras 4–6.
3. See p. 76, para. 3.   **4.** See p. 75, para. 2.
5. See p. 78, para. 2.   **6.** See p. 76, para. 6.
7. See p. 76, para. 7; p. 78, para. 1.
8. 'Charity' is often used to mean almsgiving or welfare work, but see p. 76, para. 3, and last 6 lines and p. 78, lines 1 & 2.

5.16–26

1. See p. 84, para. 2.
2. See p. 80, note on 'jealousy'; p. 82, paras 2 & 3.
3. Self-centredness, egotism, selfish ambition, introversion.
4. See p. 81, para. 2.   **5.** See p. 82, para. 2.
6. See p. 80, note on 5.22; p. 84, para. 3.
7. (a) vv. 22, 23; (b) v. 24.
8. See p. 81, last 2 paras. and p. 82, para. 1.

6.1–10

1. See p. 86, paras 3 & 4.   **2.** See p. 86, para. 5; p. 87, para. 1.
3. See p. 86, Interpretation, paras 1–3, and see also p. 62, para. 3 and p. 65, para. 2.
4. See p. 86, paras 2, 3, 5.   **5.** See p. 87, para. 3.
6. (a) v. 2; (b) v. 3.   **9.** See p. 86, para. 2.

6.11–18

1. See p. 89, note on 6.16.   **2.** See p. 89, note on 6.17.
3. This gave the letter a more personal and friendly character.
4. See p. 69, para. 5; p. 90, paras 1 & 2.   **5.** See p. 90, paras 2 & 3.
6. See p. 31, para. 5; p. 89, note on 6.14.   **8.** See p. 90, para. 4.
9. See p. 8, paras 2–3; p. 11, paras 2–5; p.82, para. 3; p.90, para. 1.
10. Take into account p. 31, para. 5, and Rom. 6.3–4.

Index

This index contains only the more important names of people and places and the main subjects occurring in the Letter to the Galatians. The names of God and Jesus, and of Paul and the Galatians, are not included as they appear on almost every page. Bold type shows where a subject is discussed in detail.